Palgrave Science Fiction and Fantasy: A New Canon

Series Editors
Anna McFarlane
Medical Humanities Research Group
University of Leeds
Dundee, UK

Timothy S. Miller
Boca Raton, USA

Palgrave Science Fiction and Fantasy: A New Canon provides short introductions to key works of science fiction and fantasy (SFF) speaking to why a text, trilogy, or series matters to SFF as a genre as well as to readers, scholars, and fans. These books aim to serve as a go-to resource for thinking on specific texts and series and for prompting further inquiry. Each book will be less than 30,000 words and structured similarly to facilitate classroom use. Focusing specifically on literature, the books will also address film and TV adaptations of the texts as relevant. Beginning with background and context on the text's place in the field, the author and how this text fits in their oeuvre, and the socio-historical reception of the text, the books will provide an understanding of how students, readers, and scholars can think dynamically about a given text. Each book will describe the major approaches to the text and how the critical engagements with the text have shaped SFF. Engaging with classic works as well as recent books that have been taken up by SFF fans and scholars, the goal of the series is not to be the arbiters of canonical importance, but to show how sustained critical analysis of these texts might bring about a new canon. In addition to their suitability for undergraduate courses, the books will appeal to fans of SFF.

Paul March-Russell

J. G. Ballard's *Crash*

palgrave
macmillan

Paul March-Russell
Independent Scholar
Canterbury, UK

ISSN 2662-8562　　　　　ISSN 2662-8570　(electronic)
Palgrave Science Fiction and Fantasy: A New Canon
ISBN 978-3-031-73093-1　　ISBN 978-3-031-73094-8　(eBook)
https://doi.org/10.1007/978-3-031-73094-8

© The Editor(s) (if applicable) and The Author(s), under exclusive license to Springer Nature Switzerland AG 2025

This work is subject to copyright. All rights are solely and exclusively licensed by the Publisher, whether the whole or part of the material is concerned, specifically the rights of translation, reprinting, reuse of illustrations, recitation, broadcasting, reproduction on microfilms or in any other physical way, and transmission or information storage and retrieval, electronic adaptation, computer software, or by similar or dissimilar methodology now known or hereafter developed.
The use of general descriptive names, registered names, trademarks, service marks, etc. in this publication does not imply, even in the absence of a specific statement, that such names are exempt from the relevant protective laws and regulations and therefore free for general use.
The publisher, the authors and the editors are safe to assume that the advice and information in this book are believed to be true and accurate at the date of publication. Neither the publisher nor the authors or the editors give a warranty, expressed or implied, with respect to the material contained herein or for any errors or omissions that may have been made. The publisher remains neutral with regard to jurisdictional claims in published maps and institutional affiliations.

This Palgrave Macmillan imprint is published by the registered company Springer Nature Switzerland AG.
The registered company address is: Gewerbestrasse 11, 6330 Cham, Switzerland

If disposing of this product, please recycle the paper.

Acknowledgements

I first of all thank the Estate of J.G. Ballard and Penguin Random House for granting me permission to access the Jonathan Cape Archive at the University of Reading Special Collections. I am also indebted to the resources of the Templeman Library, University of Kent, and to Chris Beckett of The British Library for pointing me in the right direction. This book began life as an idea in the early stages of the COVID-19 pandemic and was completed in its aftermath. I am grateful to the original series editors, Keren Omry and Sean Guynes, and their successors, Anna McFarlane and Tim Miller, as well as Brian Halm and the team at Palgrave Macmillan. Many thanks, for their advice and encouragement, to Liz Askey, Mike Bonsall, Andrew M. Butler, Felicity Dunworth, Katie Heffner, Mike Holliday, Gwyneth Jones, Paul Kincaid, Roger Luckhurst, Una McCormack, Rick McGrath, David Pringle and Will Slocombe. Parts of Chaps. 2, 3 and 4 were originally presented at university conferences at Kent and Liverpool. Writing a book about *Crash* is not for the unwary and I have been fortunate to have my own 'miracles of life' in Kirit and Marie. This book is dedicated to the memories of departed friends: Chris Priest, Maureen Kincaid Speller and Brian Stableford.

Notoriously, Ballard was involved in a car accident two weeks after submitting the manuscript of *Crash*. By strange coincidence, during the weekend I bought my copy, I was involved in a night-time collision between two New York taxi drivers, who proceeded to race one another, hurling abuse, through the city streets. No sexual pleasure was elicited, only blind terror. And yet, in a perverse way, I am grateful to those drivers for taking me that close to the spirit of *Thanatos*.

Contents

1 Introduction: *Crash* and Canonicity — 1

2 Reading *Crash*: The Making of a Modern Myth — 9

3 Writing *Crash:* Modernism/Science Fiction/*New Worlds* — 23

4 Rogue Anthropology: *Crash*, Surrealism and the Independent Group — 43

5 Body Horrors: Cyborgs, Reptiles and Mongrels — 57

6 Moral Pornography: Sex, Power and Representation — 69

7 Coda: Autogeddon/Anthropocene — 81

Index — 87

Abbreviations

AE	*The Atrocity Exhibition* (1970; London: Flamingo, 1993)
C	*Crash* (1973; New York: Vintage, 1985)
CC	Correspondence relating to the publication of *Crash* by James Graham Ballard (JC 182/3) (1972/3) File (Jonathan Cape Archive, Special Collections, University of Reading)
CCE	*Crash: The Collector's Edition*, ed. Chris Beckett (London: Fourth Estate, 2017)
DM	*Dream Makers: Science Fiction and Fantasy Writers at Work*, ed. Charles Platt, 89–96 (London: Xanadu, 1987)
DW	*The Drowned World* (1962; London: Gollancz, 2001)
EM	*Extreme Metaphors: Collected Interviews*, eds. Simon Sellars and Dan O'Hara (2012; London: Fourth Estate, 2014)
FSS	'From Shanghai to Shepperton' (with David Pringle), *Foundation* 24: 5–23
IT	*The Imagination on Trial*, eds. Alan Burns and Charles Sugnet, 15–30 (London: Allison & Busby, 1981)
KW	*The Kindness of Women* (1991; London: Grafton, 1992)
ML	*Miracles of Life* (London: Harper Perennial, 2008)
RS	*Re/Search* 8/9: J.G. Ballard, eds. V. Vale and Andrea Juno (San Francisco: Re/Search Publications, 1984)
SN	*Selected Nonfiction, 1962–2007*, ed. Mark Blacklock (Cambridge MA: MIT Press, 2023)
SW	'Some Words about *Crash!*', *Foundation* 9: 45–9
TL	'Two Letters', *Foundation* 10: 50–2
UG	*A User's Guide to the Millennium* (1996; London: Flamingo, 1997)

CHAPTER 1

Introduction: *Crash* and Canonicity

Abstract This introduction explores the various ways in which *Crash* problematises the idea of the literary canon. By drawing attention to how the novel foregrounds interpretative frameworks, it proposes that intersectionality should be the basis for 'a new canon' in SF/F. *Crash* contributes to this argument by its collision of multiple and competing discourses.

Keywords Canon • Genre • Reading protocols • Intersectionality

It was not without irony that, in 2021, Julia Ducournau's techno-horror film, *Titane*, won the Palme d'Or exactly twenty-five years after David Cronenberg's adaptation of J.G. Ballard's *Crash* (1973) had been reviled by the Cannes audience.[1] Despite Ducournau's denials, her film clearly evoked the perverse technophilia of Cronenberg's original, not least in the sexual relationship between the cyborg protagonist and her car. A year later, the electro-pop singer Charli XCX topped the UK album charts with her record entitled *Crash*, on whose cover the artist appeared semi-naked, sprawled across a cracked windshield, blood flowing from her forehead. Thus, she joined a long tradition of musicians who had taken inspiration from Ballard's novel, beginning with The Normal's 'Warm Leatherette' (1978).

© The Author(s), under exclusive license to Springer Nature Switzerland AG 2025
P. March-Russell, *J. G. Ballard's* Crash, Palgrave Science Fiction and Fantasy: A New Canon,
https://doi.org/10.1007/978-3-031-73094-8_1

But what was surprising was that these successful young artists were both invoking a novel, reviewed with disgust on its publication, years before either of them had been born. Ballard's novel is simultaneously historical and contemporary, both a source of influence and a provocation, long after the avant-garde (to which it partially belongs) had supposedly lost its effect. Quite how the novel continues to trouble and disturb is what this book examines. And it does that by considering how *Crash* operates as a fork in the crossroads of two traditions—the avant-garde and science fiction.

For the uninitiated, *Crash* marked Ballard's return to linear narrative after the non-chronological *The Atrocity Exhibition* (1970), his series of short stories or 'condensed novels' that explored the intersection between the protagonist's private fantasies—his desire to restage the deaths of John F. Kennedy and Marilyn Monroe in ways that make sense—and their enframing by the exchange systems of media, capital and data.[2] Although seemingly more conventional than its predecessor, *Crash* was a direct result: an intense exploration of the former's themes of sex, violence and mediated reality. After an accident on the recently opened London Westway, *Crash*'s narrator, an advertising agent also called James Ballard, becomes drawn to the erotic possibilities of the car crash. James initiates a love triangle between his wife Catherine and the other survivor of the accident, Helen Remington, as they explore the car's sexual geometry. However, they are being followed by Vaughan, a former computer scientist and media pundit, who believes that the car crash is the basis for a new form of sexuality where flesh and metal coincide. Vaughan, who dreams of dying in a head-on collision with the film actress Elizabeth Taylor, inveigles James into helping him and his entourage of stunt drivers and crippled women, who restage the deaths of famous car crash victims such as James Dean and Jayne Mansfield. Here is a brief sample of the imagery and prose style:

> In his vision of a car-crash with the actress, Vaughan was obsessed by many wounds and impacts – by the dying chromium and collapsing bulkheads of their two cars meeting head-on in complex collisions endlessly repeated in slow-motion films, by the identical wounds inflicted on their bodies, by the image of windshield glass frosting around her face as she broke its tinted surface like a death-born Aphrodite, by the compound fractures of their thighs impacted against their handbrake mountings, and above all by the wounds to their genitalia. (*C* 8)

We are immediately faced with a dilemma, one that is pertinent to the series in which this book appears. To what canon could *Crash* possibly belong? What canon would admit this novel, a text which from the outset declared its cult status? Or put another way, to which canon could this novel submit itself? Images of submission, acquiescence, power and its necessary corollary, violence, are rapidly invoked when we try to conceive how this novel could ever possibly be canonised. *Crash*'s taboo content; its flat, affectless prose; its very resistance to being read pose glaring questions about ideas of the canon, canonicity and canonisation. These challenges are all the more relevant for a series that proposes 'a new canon' for popular genres—science fiction and fantasy—that, although at the forefront of global cultural industries, are still viewed disdainfully by custodians of literary 'taste'. Neither mass product nor highbrow fiction, *Crash* unsettles the criteria upon which a project of re-canonisation can even be imagined. And this is what makes *Crash* significant for this series—and for the reader's understanding of science fiction's relationship to other forms of art and literature.

So, what do we mean by a 'canon'? According to the *Oxford English Dictionary*, the earliest printed use of the word is from c. 890 CE, where it referred to 'a rule, law or decree of the Church'. During the Middle Ages, it came to describe a clergyman and then the books of the Bible as authenticated by Roman Catholicism. By the end of the sixteenth century, the term had gravitated into natural philosophy where it meant 'a general rule, fundamental principle ... or axiom'; into aesthetics as 'a standard of judgement or authority'; and composition as a musical sequence where each element imitates its predecessor with slight changes in pitch or timbre. Only in the twentieth century, in the wake of World War I, did 'canon' enter literary criticism where it then described a body of works 'regarded the most important, significant and worthy of study'. So, a canon is approved by an institution; it carries authority, legality and authenticity; it is administered by an appointed representative; it appears to be immutable; it acts as a cultural marker; it is sequential, ordered and respectful of tradition (albeit with minor variations); and it is culturally valuable: it makes demands of the uninitiated who, by their hard work, will join the Elect. As such, canon-formation is inherently a political act. Despite the appearance of immutability, canons are man-made and consequently describe an approved version of culture, history and knowledge. Not for nothing, then, that during the 1970s and 1980s literary canons came under scrutiny from proletarian, feminist, and postcolonial perspectives.

This current series is symptomatic of a moment when, on the one hand, the curriculum is being decolonised according to ethnic, gendered, queer and disabled critiques, whilst on the other hand, those same approaches are being assailed as examples of 'cancel culture' led by 'woke' universities. As recent controversies, such as Racefail and the Rabid Puppies, indicate, SF/F is not immune from these same crises. To propose the very idea of a canon, let alone a 'new' canon, is politically sensitive.

Crash, though, is an ideal text to think through these tensions since, as 'the first pornographic novel based on technology', it 'has a political role quite apart from its sexual content' (*C* 6). At first glance, however, my claim for *Crash* may appear strange since, unlike other decolonising texts, it is written by a white, middle-class, heterosexual Englishman, living in suburbia, raised in the colonial outpost of Shanghai, and compelled by his own deeply masculine obsessions with media and technology. It is precisely the extremity, though, to which Ballard was compelled that makes *Crash* such a difficult text to categorise and canonise. The unruliness of *Crash*, despite or even because of its cool tonal register, makes the novel ideal for thinking through the rules—the political and institutional choices—that govern canon-formation. To reintroduce *Crash* into the equation is to potentially explode the idea of the canon and the frameworks that permit its existence.

Consequently, I am especially concerned with how we read the novel. Roger Luckhurst (1997, xiii), drawing upon the terminology of Jacques Derrida, has recounted how Ballard's fiction acts as a 'hinge' within the SF genre: 'the point in any structural system that makes the working of the system at once possible and impossible'. The extent to which Ballard's fiction 're-marks' upon the genre, first, by drawing attention to its status as science fiction; second, by reversing our narrative expectations; third, by reiterating Ballard's own narrative tropes; and last, by foregrounding the role of zones and borderlines, emphasises the illusion of generic purity (Luckhurst 1997, 30–6). Ballard is simultaneously both inside and outside the genre: to attempt to position him one way or the other institutes a border that Ballard's fiction actively dissolves. The ebb and flow of Ballard's prose is exemplified, in a later essay by Luckhurst, by an incantatory passage that nonetheless veers upon the comic: why, Luckhurst (2005, 516) asks, 'do *lesbian* manageresses drive *midget* cars and die in front of *middle-aged* firemen?' These seemingly redundant adjectives appear to undermine a fantasy of horrific violence. In 2016, following the deposit of Ballard's manuscripts at the British Library, Luckhurst acknowledges it is now possible to trace how precisely Ballard strove in his choice of language for an 'unnerving balance of documentary and absurdity'. Such fastidiousness, though, is also adept at undermining the attempts of literary critics to reclaim the text from postmodern appropriations through the value-laden practice of close reading.[3] In such an instance, paying strict attention to the word may actually lead us astray; to recapitulate an absurd loss of meaning already inherent in Ballard's language use.

Following Luckhurst, I explore how *Crash* exposes both reading protocols and frames of reference, not as an escape from Ballard's science fiction roots, but as an effect of its generic origins. However, whereas Luckhurst (2005, 520) ultimately turns to a contextualisation of the novel 'in all the complexity of its place in science fiction history and the explosive cultural-historical milieux of England in the early 1970s,' I adopt a slightly different tack by focusing upon its mode of production. The novel was the outcome of a long gestation that included other creative acts: short stories, an art exhibition, a proposed performance piece, a TV drama-documentary. These parts in a creative process, whereby Ballard came to regard the car crash as 'a total metaphor for man's life in today's society' (*C* 6), were indivisible from the mounting financial chaos of *New Worlds* magazine and the collapse of the New Wave in science fiction, of which *Crash* was its apotheosis. To understand one is to understand the other. Ballard's private motivations, though, emerge in his correspondence with his publisher, Tom Maschler, and their mutual desires to derive a bestseller from this seemingly unpropitious material. The largely hostile reaction of *Crash*'s initial reviewers, and the novel's subsequent success in France, add to its mythology as a cult classic whilst also paving the way for its entanglement in the rise of postmodern culture during the 1990s. In resistance to this appropriation, I take the novel's construction back to its origins, alongside science fiction, within the post-war legacy of surrealism, chiefly within the British Pop Art movement represented by the Independent Group. From there, I explore the novel's affinities with anthropological research, the posthuman reclamation of the animalistic, and Ballard's defence of pornography as a political art-form. The fact that the novel can positively intersect with these seemingly non-science-fictional discourses, without betraying its SF roots, is testimony to how Ballard constantly challenges frames of reference. What he offers instead is a science fiction novel that is both interdisciplinary and intersectional at the same time. Over and above the graphic sex and violence of the novel, it is this quality—at once transcendent and immanent of science fiction—that arguably causes its readers both so much distress and so much awe.

It is also why we should now be thinking of *Crash* in terms of 'a new canon', even while taking into account the tensions surrounding canonicity outlined above. Although D. Harlan Wilson (2017, 83) has criticized the undue prominence given to the decade from the first of Ballard's condensed novels in 1966 to his collection *Low-Flying Aircraft* (1976), in more recent years, greater critical attention has been paid to the global catastrophe novels of the 1960s and the late dystopias from 1996 to 2006. Both tendencies have effectively been attempts at canonising Ballard: as a precursor to either the sub-genre of climate fiction or the twenty-first century boom in dystopian fiction.[4] For non-SF readers, Ballard may be better known for his quasi-autobiographical novel, *Empire of the Sun* (1984), in which case he might be read alongside a canon of other British authors preoccupied with decolonisation, amongst them, Anthony Burgess, J.G. Farrell, Graham Greene and Muriel Spark. Yet, *Empire of the Sun* and its sequel, *The Kindness of Women* (1991), are still marked by the stylistic and thematic concerns that characterise Ballard's SF, including that of *Crash* and the urban catastrophes, *Concrete Island* (1974) and *High-Rise* (1975). In whichever way we approach Ballard's career, we still come back to the fictions of his middle period since they most embody his troubling relationship to genre and, hence, his problematising of canonicity. If we are committed to conceiving 'a new canon' for SF and fantasy, then Ballard's works, most notably *Crash*, act as a litmus test for this re-conceptualisation.

In particular, I would argue that intersectionality characterises the 'newness' of this speculative canon. First proposed in 1989 by the legal scholar, Kimberlé Crenshaw (although predated by such other civil rights activists as Angela Davis), intersectionality has typified Fourth Wave feminism's response to the question of women's rights as entangled with other socio-cultural issues: race, class, gender, ability, amongst them. It is perhaps not entirely coincident that the concept of intersectionality emerged just as the social impact of the World Wide Web was about to break, as witnessed by such prophetic texts as Manuel Castells's *The Rise of the Network Society* (1996). Although Caroline Edwards (2019, 119–31) has proposed a more recent sub-genre of what she terms 'networked novels', including texts by Joanna Kavenna, Hari Kunzru and David Mitchell, the notion of networking is already evident in *The Atrocity Exhibition*. Furthermore, *Crash* shares with its predecessor the intersecting of multiple discourses, which although different from the kind of intersectionality proposed by Fourth Wave feminism, nonetheless prefigures the networking of information that we are now familiar with. The potential overload of data adds significantly to the difficulty of reading *Crash*, but it also marks the novel as being in step with more recent SF, whether that be post-cyberpunk or New Space Opera, where the informational excess is part of the textual effect. Consequently, although seemingly very different from its successors, *Crash* is a key, albeit disruptive, element to what we might term 'a new canon' in SF.

To unlock that mystery, though, we must first turn to how *Crash* has been read and re-read. For the mythology of Ballard's disturbing, enigmatic text began the very moment he submitted it to his publisher in February 1972.

Notes

1. Quite distinct from Ballard's novel, there is already a large body of criticism on Cronenberg's film version. A freewheeling introduction is offered by Sinclair (1999). For a more measured response, see Ruddick (2016, 239–50). On the scandal surrounding the film's delayed release in the UK, see Barker et al. (2001).
2. For many Ballardians, *The Atrocity Exhibition* is his masterpiece. There is consequently substantial scholarship on this text. See, for example, March-Russell (2011).
3. In this respect, compare Day's (2000) flawed but well-intentioned attempt with what a close reading can achieve, based on the draft manuscripts held at the British Library (Beckett 2016).
4. For accounts that problematise these approaches, see respectively Clarke (2013) and Wood (2012).

Works Cited

Barker, Martin, et al. 2001. *The Crash Controversy: Censorship Campaigns and Film Reception*. London: Wallflower Press.

Beckett, Chris. 2016. The Opening of *Crash* in Slow Motion. https://www.bl.uk/20th-century-literature/articles/the-opening-of-crash-in-slow-motion (accessed 19/03/23).

Clarke, Jim. 2013. Reading Climate Change in J.G. Ballard. *Critical Survey* 25 (2): 7–21.

Day, Aidan. 2000. Ballard and Baudrillard: Close Reading *Crash*. *English* 49: 277–293.
Edwards, Caroline. 2019. *Utopia and the Contemporary British Novel*. Cambridge: Cambridge University Press.
Luckhurst, Roger. 1997. *'The Angle Between Two Walls': The Fiction of J.G. Ballard*. Liverpool: Liverpool University Press.
———. 2005. J.G. Ballard: *Crash*. In *A Companion to Science Fiction*, ed. David Seed, 512–521. Oxford: Blackwell.
———. 2016. An Introduction to *Crash*. https://www.bl.uk/20th-century-literature/articles/an-introduction-to-crash (accessed 19/03/23).
March-Russell, Paul. 2011. Exploding the Open Book: *The Atrocity Exhibition*, *Vermilion Sands* and the Ethics of the Short Story Cycle. *Short Fiction in Theory and Practice* 1 (1): 95–108.
Ruddick, Nicholas. 2016. *Science Fiction Adapted to Film*. Canterbury: Gylphi.
Sinclair, Iain. 1999. *Crash: David Cronenberg's Post-Mortem on J.G. Ballard's 'Trajectory of Fate'*. London: BFI Publishing.
Wilson, D. Harlan. 2017. *J.G. Ballard*. Urbana: University of Illinois Press.
Wood, John Carter. 2012. "Going mad is their only way of staying sane": Norbert Elias and the Civilised Violence of J.G. Ballard. In *J.G. Ballard: Visions and Revisions*, ed. Jeannette Baxter and Rowland Wymer, 198–214. Basingstoke: Palgrave Macmillan.

CHAPTER 2

Reading *Crash*: The Making of a Modern Myth

Abstract This chapter argues that, even before it was published, *Crash* had acquired a mythic status. This quality was not only generated by how the novel was read and re-read but it has also sustained *Crash*'s longevity and prevalence within contemporary culture. The chapter offers a history of how the novel has been received, from the original correspondence between Ballard and his publisher to the initial outcry of its reviewers, from its appropriation by post-punk musicians and postmodern theory to its influence on the visual arts and transhumanism.

Keywords Reception • Post-punk • Jean Baudrillard • Postmodernism
• Academia

Crash's mythic allure began with the reported response of its first professional reader. Speaking in 1974, Ballard commented:

> One of the publisher's readers was either a psychiatrist or the wife of a psychiatrist, and she wrote the most damning and vituperative reader's report they'd ever received. It included the statement: 'The author is beyond psychiatric help'. … But I was quite pleased by the report, because it represents, in a sense, total artistic success. The book had *worked* if somebody could respond like that to it. (*IT* 22–3)

© The Author(s), under exclusive license to Springer Nature
Switzerland AG 2025
P. March-Russell, *J. G. Ballard's* Crash, Palgrave Science Fiction
and Fantasy: A New Canon,
https://doi.org/10.1007/978-3-031-73094-8_2

Despite Ballard's vagueness as to their identity, the reader in question was Catherine Peters, the second wife of the psychiatrist Anthony Storr and a Senior Reader at Jonathan Cape. Under her maiden name, Peters subsequently became a lecturer at Somerville College, Oxford, and an expert on Wilkie Collins, Charles Dickens and W.M. Thackeray. Storr himself was a Jungian analyst and author of books with strangely Ballardian themes: *Sexual Deviation* (1964), *Human Aggression* (1968) and *Human Destructiveness* (1972). In *The Dynamics of Creation* (1972), Storr argued that these perverse and violent desires could be sublimated into artistic creativity. Although there is no evidence that Ballard read Storr's books, he may have seen them reviewed. Even more curiously, Storr's first wife, also called Catherine, was the celebrated children's writer of the disturbing supernatural tale, *Marianne Dreams* (1958), televised on British TV in 1972 as *Escape into Night*. We can even imagine Ballard sitting down to watch this with his own children.

By the time that the composer and musician Graeme Revell had interviewed Ballard in 1983, the words 'DO NOT PUBLISH' had been appended to the report (*RS* 144). The story of Peters's reaction has been repeated endlessly, cementing the novel's transgressive appeal. However, if Ballard dined out on the response, it has also been amplified by critics. Matthew Sterenberg (2011, 257) concocts an entire scenario when he writes:

> In 1973 a manuscript reviewer for a major British publishing firm sat horrified by what she was reading. As she turned the pages she grew increasingly disturbed by the tale of a group of Londoners who are sexually fascinated by car crashes. The wife of a prominent psychiatrist, she was certain the manuscript was the product of a mind that was utterly deranged. What she was reading was not a novel at all; it was evidence of hopeless psychopathology.

Ironically, for an article concerned with the role of myth in post-war science fiction, this is itself an exercise in myth-making: for starters, *Crash* was submitted to Jonathan Cape in 1972, not 1973. Instead, research in the Jonathan Cape Archive at the University of Reading reveals that Peters's written report does not exist. Tom Maschler, Ballard's publisher, was the book's first reader and he reports as having been 'knocked over by its impact' (*CC*, 5 April 1972). Wisely though, Maschler shared the manuscript not only with Peters but also several other readers, some of whom loved it, some of whom hated it, but all of whom thought it was 'too long' (*CC*, 3 May 1972).

Writing in 2010, Mike Petty, the novel's copyeditor, recalled the 'controversy' that surrounded *Crash* 'from the moment it arrived on Tom Mascher's desk'.[1] Petty refers to a report having existed and that Peters 'didn't think' the book 'should be published'. He suggests, though, that Ballard overstated its 'significance' and that Senior Readers would 'say this sort of thing all the time – this guy's a nutter, we should notify the police, etc.' Whereas Ballard emphasises the uniqueness of Peters's outburst, Petty also remarks that she similarly objected to Martin Amis's *The Rachel Papers* (1973), which Cape published just five months after *Crash*. Petty's account is corroborated by the writer Emma Tennant (1999, 1), who was presented with a proof copy of *Crash* by Michael Dempsey, an editor at Granada that also published Ballard, and noted that it was 'material so toxic that a reader at the publisher Jonathan Cape has pronounced its creator fit for psychiatric treatment'. However, while Tennant's recollection seems to authenticate the wording attributed to Peters, it also indicates that this yet unpublished novel was already the subject of rumour and gossip. By contrast, Maschler states that he would 'unconditionally' publish *Crash* but recommends shortening it so as to avoid the novel being 'too expensive' (*CC*, 3 May 1972).

Whereas academic criticism offers increasingly abstract theorisations of *Crash*, a more materialistic picture emerges from Ballard's correspondence with Maschler. Ballard emphasises that he is 'almost broke' and desperate for a 'sales breakthrough' (*CC*, 10 April 1972). More than once, Ballard asks for his advance so that he can feed both himself and his family. Since the death of his wife Mary in 1964, Ballard had been a single father to his three young children and earned his living solely through his writing. Novels such as *The Drowned World* (1963) and *The Crystal World* (1966) had been moderate successes and Ballard had received support from significant critics, most notably Kingsley Amis, as well as opprobrium from US genre reviewers. But *The Atrocity Exhibition* (1970) had proved disastrous in the US: Doubleday, scared at the possibility of legal action because of Ballard's use of real-life personalities, withdrew the book and pulped the remaining copies; E.P. Dutton took fright for similar reasons; and it was not until 1972 that it was republished in the US by Grove Press under a title that Ballard disliked (*Love and Napalm: Export U.S.A.*). Ballard's mounting financial problems were compounded by his anxiety for the safety of his children. The eastern section of the M3 motorway, incomplete until 1974, was being built close to where Ballard lived in Shepperton. Everyday his young family had to negotiate increasingly busy roads: 'I didn't want a knock on the door and see a bobby or a policewoman come to tell me some unpleasant news. That really would have been life's most bitter joke' (*FSS* 22). No wonder then that, in his 1974 introduction to the French edition of *Crash*, Ballard remarked: 'what our children have to fear is not the cars on the highways of tomorrow but our own pleasure in calculating the most elegant parameters of their deaths' (*C* 1).[2]

Ballard expressed his desperation at this time in his 1993 radio interview with Mick Brown (itself sampled by the Manic Street Preachers for their 1994 album *The Holy Bible*):

> I wanted to write a book where there was nowhere to hide. It would have been very easy to write a cautionary tale about the dangers of driving too fast, having sex with underage girls in the back seats of cars, or whatever. I didn't want to write that sort of book at all. I wanted to rub the human face in its own vomit, then force it to look in the mirror. (Brown 1993)

But in 1972, Ballard still had to pitch his novel to his publisher. Writing to Maschler, he emphasises its topicality, alluding to a recent spate of motorway accidents and the alarming statistics on road safety. But unlike campaigners such as Ralph Nader, whom Ballard regarded as an 'opportunist using the psychological weaponry of fear and anxiety' (*UG* 259), Ballard proposed to Maschler that '*Crash* takes these deaths and injuries as an extreme metaphor for the whole future of sex and technology' (*CC*, 7 April 1972). Yet, although Ballard stressed the 'moral urgency' of his investigation, he nonetheless hoped 'to offend' critics, and to appeal to the filmgoers of such recent controversies as *The Wild Bunch* (1969), *Straw Dogs* and *A Clockwork Orange* (both 1971). Three days later, Ballard asked Maschler if the novel could 'achieve success as a result of its sensational qualities … in short as a terrifying cautionary tale?' (*CC*, 10 April 1972). Whether or not Ballard wrote the novel as a caution is irrelevant: what is significant is that, in responding to Maschler, Ballard was himself re-reading the novel with an eye to the market. Having previously mentioned movies, Ballard now compares *Crash* to such cult novels as Jean Genet's *Our Lady of the Flowers* (1943), Malcolm Lowry's *Under the Volcano* (1947), Pauline Réage's *Story of O* (1954) and William Burroughs's *Naked Lunch* (1959), novels 'detested to begin with', marked by 'long passages of boredom', yet which 'get through to the reader by their total obsessiveness' and 'grim logic'. With a marketing strategy now starting to emerge, Ballard readily agreed to Maschler's advice to cut the text. As Maschler acknowledged, it was 'difficult ... to evaluate' *Crash*'s chances for commercial success but he urged Ballard on: 'we will win through' (*CC*, 8 June 1972).

Ballard submitted his revised manuscript four months later. He had in fact gone further than Maschler's advice and had removed 25–30% of the text (dozens of excised pages are to be found in the Jonathan Cape Archive). Ballard observed that this material was overlong, 'difficult to follow', 'repetitive' and an 'elaboration of violent detail' amounting to 'pure sermonising'. Instead, 'at approximately 70,000 words it should read like a blow in the face' with now 'a natural balance between the actions of the narrator and his own interiorised obsession' (*CC*, 8 October 1972). Crucially then, in stripping back his manuscript, Ballard not only enforced its shock effect—an avant-garde technique that Ballard not only associated with the surrealists but also filmmakers such as Stanley Kubrick and Sam Peckinpah—but he also strengthened the moral ambiguity of the narration. In his original pitch, Ballard claimed that his intention 'was to be honest' (*CC*, 7 April 1972), which is why he had called his first-person narrator James Ballard, to indicate his own complicity in a 'sexual experience that we secretly desire' (*CC*, 10 April 1972). Now this honesty was all the more unsettling because Ballard had removed any lasting trace of his own authorial voice in the text.

Mike Petty was possibly chosen to copyedit *Crash* because he was then the only male copyeditor at Jonathan Cape. He acknowledged its completion with the following note: 'I can't say I enjoyed working on it much, but then I don't suppose I was meant to. In fact, I found it a thoroughly frightening and disturbing experience' (*CC*, 14 December 1972). Since it's impossible to know just what Peters wrote—the wording, as we have it, is solely Ballard's—Petty's letter may stand as a substitute; indeed, it may have even informed Ballard's recollection of the lost report. The only other key change occurred at the proofing stage on 24 February 1973, when Ballard decided to drop the exclamation mark from the title (although retained for the French edition). The last act of framing the text came in the form of its jacket design by Bill Botten: a long pink gear-stick, obviously phallic, backed by the title in giant letters 'in metallic silver with spongy flesh tissue behind' (*CC*, 12 January 1973). Praised by Ballard at the time, 'A brilliant jacket, congratulate the artist for me' (*CC*, 21 March

1973), he later called it 'monstrously bad, one of the worst book jackets ever—for sheer ugliness and crudity, impossible to beat' (Poynor 2004). The accompanying blurb was written by Ballard himself, derived from the synopsis in his letter written to Maschler on 10 April 1972.

Peters's fabled report has created a mythical origin story for Ballard's novel, a shorthand which, whatever the reader's intention, has served to both market *Crash* as an archetypal cult fiction and to signify its transgressiveness. By diminishing the report and focusing instead on the Cape correspondence, it is possible to see how the manuscript was read and re-read, resulting not only in major revisions but also the greater ambiguity of the finished work. These changes were done in the hope of commercial success, trading both upon the novel's graphic content and its comparison with other sensational texts, whether that be current controversies, such as Kubrick's *A Clockwork Orange*, or a lineage of transgressive fictions. Instead, the novel's reception ironically confirmed it as a work 'detested to begin with'.[3]

Although there was controversy when *Crash* was published in June 1973, it failed to ignite book sales as much as Ballard and Maschler had hoped. Instead, in the US and the UK, it sold no more than Ballard's previous novels, perhaps because he was still regarded as a genre writer. The minor scandal did not dent his core audience but neither did it substantially attract new readers from outside SF. The reaction can perhaps be best summed-up by Auberon Waugh's concluding remarks to his *Evening Standard* review headlined as 'Too Shocking for Words' (3 July 1973): 'the overall effect is so disgusting that I can only recommend the book to those who enjoy being disgusted'. Other pithy responses came from Myrna Blumberg in *The Times* ('repellent'), Robert Nye in *The Guardian* ('hellish'), Derek Stanford in *The Scotsman* ('revolting and vicious'), Julian Symons in *The Sunday Times* ('nastily self-indulgent') and B.A. Young in *The Financial Times* ('powerfully unpleasant'). Several reviewers made nervous plays on the word 'autoerotic', implying their deep unease with the novel, whilst others tried to dismiss it out of hand: 'a crashing bore' (*Publisher's Weekly*). Still others echoed the novel's visceral effect: 'a whiplash impact' (*Kirkus Review*); 'one long unmodulated scream' (Katherine Braverman, *Los Angeles Times*); 'perhaps Mr Ballard ... will feel better now that he has vomited this effort from his system' (John Boland, *Books and Bookmen*). All of these reviews characterised the novel, and sometimes the author, as abject and to be distanced: 'the most repulsive book I've yet to come across' (D.K. Mano, *New York Times*).

The overall effect of this reaction was, as the anonymous reviewer in *The Economist* observed, to guarantee *Crash*'s recommendation 'as a cult book': not what Ballard or Maschler were looking for in terms of sales but confirmation that *Crash* would endure as a slow-burn. There were also positive reviews amidst the backlash. Anthony Quinton in *The Sunday Telegraph* compared Ballard to John Milton, Gabriel García Márquez and Arthur Rimbaud: 'with its force and enthusiasm it redeems, rather than condemns, the wasteland it describes'. Martin Seymour-Smith in *The Observer Magazine* described *Crash* as 'one of the more outstanding of recent warnings against the dehumanised emotion and brutality that are part and parcel of the new technology'. Perhaps unexpectedly, Virginia Osborne in *Cosmopolitan* seemed to approve: 'stunningly violent and powerful', 'a very good book to give to a demon-lover'. Less surprisingly, *Playboy* wrote 'it's hard not to get caught up in this verbal acid trip with its minatory vision of the sex-technology mystique'. Two of the most attentive reviews, though, were ultimately negative ones. Valentine Cunningham in *The Listener* observed that '*Crash* enjoys the fantasies of autogeddon too much to be able to mount any but the feeblest of resistances to the car-obsessed society that makes them so available'. In *The Observer*, Martin Amis displayed his homework by listing how many times certain words had been used: 'perverse' (16 times), 'geometry' (21 times), 'stylised' (26 times). He concluded: 'In science fiction Ballard had a tight framework for his unnerving ideas, out on the lunatic fringe, he can only flail and shout'.[4] Amis's claim that Ballard had abandoned SF (and hence rationality) was mirrored by the attempts of other reviewers to categorise *Crash*: pornography, fantasy, magic realism, crime. Maxim Jakubowski in *New Scientist* reversed Amis's criticism altogether, praising *Crash* because it was 'not a work of sf'. On the other hand, in his *Foundation* review, David Pringle (1974, 86) not only made the case for *Crash* to be read as SF, where the car acts as a microcosm of a technologically saturated society, but also (despite some reservations) commended Ballard as 'the only sf writer who faces up consciously to this collective masochism of our time'.

Undeterred, Ballard quickly followed *Crash* with *Concrete Island* (1974) and *High-Rise* (1975), novels that confirmed him as the principal analyst of the urban sprawl and its underlying psychodynamics. Ballard's triptych perfectly complemented the late Situationist rhetoric of counter-cultural magazines, such as *Suburban Press*, whose fifth issue in 1972 bore a photomontage by Jamie Reid of Coventry's sprawling highways with the caption: 'Lo! A Monster is Born'. The emerging scenes of punk and post-punk, industrial rock and synth-pop frequently cited Ballard as a reference-point (Reynolds 2005). In 1978, Ballard was interviewed for the punk fanzine *Search & Destroy*, where Ballard's interest in 'a new conceptualisation of psychopathology' and 'a real liberation of the apparently deviant' (*EM* 119) seemed to coincide with the punk ethos of shock, outrage and non-conformity. Crucially, *Search & Destroy* was published by V. Vale whose next venture, Re/Search, published books by and about Ballard alongside titles on William Burroughs, industrial culture, pornography, body art, freaks and radical feminism. Vale's maverick Californian imprint complemented Sylvère Lotringer's New York-based press, Semiotext(e), which disseminated French philosophers, such as Jean Baudrillard, Gilles Deleuze, Michel Foucault and Paul Virilio, to an American audience.

Re/Search and Semiotext(e) formed an intersection between the fall-out of post-punk and industrial music and the emergence of postmodern thought in its Continental European guise. Although the impact upon Anglophone readers of Baudrillard's essay on *Crash* was not fully felt until its translation in 1991, Jonathan Benison had already registered its significance in an article published in *Foundation* in 1984: the year also that William Gibson's *Neuromancer* was published and cyberpunk, heavily indebted to Ballard, went mainstream. If the post-punk movements had established *Crash* as a cult novel, then Baudrillard's intervention seized it for academic respectability, much to Ballard's chagrin: 'Leave us be! Turn your "intelligence" to the iconography of filling stations, cash machines, or whatever nonsense your entertainment culture deems to be the flavour of the day' (*SN* 304).

Not unlike Edgar Allan Poe before him, it was the French who reclaimed Ballard and sold *Crash* back to Anglophone readers as an avatar of postmodernism. On its release in France in 1974, the novel sold over 30,000 copies—more than its combined sales in the UK and the US. Perhaps Ballard's comparisons with Genet and Réage had proved correct, and the novel had appealed to a long tradition of transgressive fictions in the French language (noting also that *Naked Lunch* had originally been published by the Paris-based Olympia Press). But New Wave SF had already found a home in France—besides such local products as the films of Jean-Luc Godard, Chris Marker and Roger Vadim, Philippe Druillet's comic-book creation Lone Sloane was influenced by Michael Moorcock's tales of the Eternal Champion. In 1975, Druillet alongside Jean Giraud (Moebius) co-founded the magazine *Métal Hurlant*, whose graphic design fed back into such US films as *Alien* (1979) and *Blade Runner* (1982).

Prior to its French publication, Ballard wrote an introduction that constituted another repositioning of the novel. Whilst the long defence of science fiction was largely lifted from his 1969 essay about Salvador Dalí, 'The Innocent as Paranoid', many of the key phrases and sentiments had been rehearsed in interviews and reviews whilst Ballard was writing the original draft between December 1969 and February 1972, as well as his commentary for Harley Cokeliss's short drama-documentary *Crash!* (1971). To these elements, Ballard added parts from the jacket blurb he wrote for the first UK hardback edition, which concluded: 'the ultimate role of *Crash* is cautionary, a warning against that brutal, erotic and overlit realm that beckons more and more persuasively from the margins of the technological landscape' (*C* 6). There has been much discussion as to what Ballard meant by 'cautionary', a word that he had originally introduced in his correspondence with Maschler. Speaking in 1974, Ballard distinguished between 'cautionary' and 'moral': 'there's nothing moral about shouting, "Careful, there's a car coming"' (*IT* 21). Interviewed by Catherine Bresson eight years later, Ballard reflected: 'I was not altogether honest in this introduction because I did imply that there was a ... moral dimension which I don't really think is there' (quoted Benison 1984, 41). By 1994, Ballard claimed that '*Crash* was not a cautionary tale' but 'a psychopathic hymn which has a point' (Self 1995, 348). This 'point' he later enumerated as Swiftian satire that 'seems to embrace the very subject' of its 'anger' and 'removes the moral framework that reassures the spectator' (Hultkrans 1997, 78).[5] Although the allusion to Jonathan Swift may be another way that Ballard sought to distance the novel from SF, he effectively reiterates what he first proposed in 1975: that, in writing *Crash*, Ballard 'chose to completely accept the demands of the subject matter ... in order to provoke' and 'test' the reader (Goddard and Pringle 1976, 46).

The problem though with such a cool, straight-faced approach is that it can be taken literally—which is what Baudrillard does. Although not included in the original English translation of *Simulacra and Simulation* (1981), Baudrillard's essay on *Crash* was the first segment to be published in 1976. Three years before, in *The Mirror of Production* (1973), Baudrillard had completed his break with classical Marxist theory, and in *Symbolic Exchange and Death* (1976), had introduced his more characteristic rhetoric of hyperreality: 'the real is not only that which can be reproduced, but *that which is always already reproduced*' (Baudrillard 1993, 73).[6] As Ballard puts it, a world governed 'by fictions of every kind' so that 'any free or original imaginative response to experience' is anticipated by mass media, advertising and consumerism (*C* 5) consists solely of a pre-packaged illusion. For Baudrillard (1991, 319), *Crash* proves his thesis that 'there is neither fiction nor reality – a kind of hyperreality has abolished both'. As a consequence, the novel defies criticism and, for the most part, Baudrillard merely recapitulates its action: the profane, desensitised and non-erotic round of sex, violence and physical wounds. Except, he also feeds that description through the conceptual language already established in *Symbolic Exchange and Death*, such that Ballard's novel is effectively assimilated into Baudrillard's own worldview. The *Crash* essay was intrinsic to the development of Baudrillard's thought but it reveals very little about the novel because it purposely takes at face value what Ballard's compromised first-person narrator has to say. Baudrillard (1991, 318) recounts at length the lack of sexual desire, a 'functionalism' that 'devours its own rationality', but fails to engage with what that signifies: the novel's 'death of affect' (*C* 1).

When Baudrillard's essay was finally translated, in *Science Fiction Studies* in 1991, it sparked furious debate within the accompanying forum of SF critics. Most productively, N. Katharine Hayles (1991, 323) emphasised that, whereas Baudrillard foregrounds the novel as an empty, immanent circuit of exchanged body parts, *Crash*'s 'erotic transformations are expressions precisely of a drive toward transcendence that does in fact culminate in flight, a flight to death'. More savagely, Vivian Sobchack (1991, 329) wished 'a little pain (maybe a lot)' on Baudrillard 'to bring him to his senses, to remind him that he has a body, *his* body, and that the "moral gaze" begins there'. Despite these responses though, as postmodernism swept through arts and humanities departments in the 1990s as a critical shibboleth, Ballard and Baudrillard were often conjoined.[7] Larry McCaffrey featured significant extracts from both authors in his seminal casebook of postmodern science fiction, *Storming the Reality Studio* (1991). Scott Bukatman (1993, 46) went further by arguing that the postmodern (despite being already common currency amongst historians, sociologists and cultural critics by the mid-1950s) was 'inconceivable' without Ballard; a view reinforced by Julian Murphet (2005, 721), who regarded *Crash* as 'Britain's great inaugural contribution to Postmodernist fiction', thereby erasing such authors as John Fowles and B.S. Johnson, let alone a host of female innovators such as Christine Brooke-Rose, Anna Kavan and Ann Quin. One of the key problems with this reading of Ballard was that it relied either upon a limited historical knowledge of science fiction, such that *Crash* was reduced to merely acting as the wet-nurse for the then voguish phenomenon of cyberpunk, or made no mention of science fiction at all. Admittedly, this dilemma was not helped by Ballard's own tendency to disregard *Crash* as SF and by his subsequent turn in the mid-1990s to the anti-detective novels of his final decade.

Roger Luckhurst's *'The Angle Between Two Walls': The Fiction of J.G. Ballard* (1997) inaugurated a more sophisticated academic approach towards reading Ballard. Although Luckhurst's aim was to show how Ballard's fiction resists generic classification, whilst still drawing strength from its roots in SF, the cumulative effect was to open Ballard up to the resources of critical theory. Since Luckhurst's book, any number of theoretical approaches have been applied to Ballard's work including *Crash*, ranging from Michel Foucault and Julia Kristeva to Jacques Lacan and Gilles Deleuze to Donna Haraway and Quentin Meillassoux.[8] Whether they are effective or not, these approaches are symptomatic of an academic industry in which literary texts are fed through critical theories to produce quantifiable research outcomes. Or, as Ballard put it in his response to the *Science Fiction Studies* roundtable: 'bourgeoisification in the form of an overprofessionalised academia' (*SN* 304). Consequently, despite their apparent assimilation to an academic treadmill, novels such as *Crash* have continued to appeal to countercultural elements: from techno-fetishist magazines such as *Mondo 2000* (1984–1998) and Warwick University's para-academic Cybernetic Culture Research Unit (1995–2003) to artists such as Mike Nelson and the 2010 exhibition, *Crash: Homage to J.G. Ballard*, at the Gagosian Gallery. At the same time, much of the most serious archival work has been done by Ballard enthusiasts, most notably, Mike Bonsall, Mike Holliday, Rick McGrath, David Pringle and Simon Sellars. Spearheaded by Jeannette Baxter in the 2000s, a younger generation of academics has moved away from theory to focus more upon the sources of Ballard's artistic practice.

Ballard's claim that 'the writer knows nothing any longer' and can only offer 'a set of options and imaginative alternatives' (*C* 5) sums up the history of reading and mythmaking in *Crash*. As Susan Sontag (1994, 16) has argued of writers and composers such as Samuel Beckett and John Cage: 'A person who becomes silent becomes opaque for the other; somebody's silence opens up an array of possibilities for interpreting that silence, for imputing speech to it.' In withdrawing his own authorial position, Ballard rendered his text opaque. This negative response, whilst at the same time galvanising his audiences' reaction (so that *Crash* becomes a text to be spoken about, to be spoken of), is arguably a characteristic modernist manoeuvre. To understand the making of *Crash*, we now need to contextualise its production within the avant-garde scene of the 1960s and *New Worlds* magazine in particular.

Notes

1. Mike Petty, private email correspondence to David Pringle (9 October 2010). I am grateful to David for sharing this information with me.
2. Editions of the novel published since the mid-1990s offer an abridged version of the introduction. The full text can also be found in *CCE*, *SN* and *SW*.
3. All quotations from reviews of *Crash* are from the folder in the Jonathan Cape Archive, catalogued as: 'Review file for *Crash* by J.G. Ballard' (RC/2/9) (1973) File.
4. It is worth noting, however, that Amis subsequently changed his view of the novel (Amis 1996).
5. In addition, some of *Crash*'s initial reviewers compared the novel to Swift. However, although Andrew M. Butler (2012, 210–1) supports Ballard's judgement, Mark Fisher (2004) regards it as 'disingenuous' on Ballard's part.
6. The term 'hyperrealism', though, did not originate with Baudrillard. It was coined in 1973 by the art dealer Isy Brachot to refer to artists who used photographs as their source material rather than the external reality. It was quickly adopted by intellectuals such as Jean-François Lyotard and Umberto Eco. Crucially though, whereas Eco maintains a distinction between the hyperrealist 'fakery' of Disneyland and a residual reality, Baudrillard collapses the distinction altogether. Disneyland, in Baudrillard's model, disguises the unreality that is the rest of the US. Contrast Baudrillard (1988, 55–6) with Eco (1987, 39–48).
7. For a pertinent critique, especially with regards to Baudrillard's reading of Ballard, see Durham (1998), 49–75.
8. See, respectively, Duffy (2016), Whiting (2012), Foster (1993), Vanhanen (2019), McQueen (2011), and Wenaus (2016).

Works Cited

Amis, Martin. 1996. Cronenberg's Monster. *The Independent on Sunday* (10 November): 8–9.

Baudrillard, Jean. 1988 (1986). *America*. Trans. Chris Turner. London: Verso.

———. 1991 (1976). Ballard's *Crash*. Trans. Arthur B. Evans. *Science Fiction Studies* 18 (3): 313–20.

———. 1993 (1976). *Symbolic Exchange and Death*. Trans. Iain Hamilton Grant. London: SAGE.
Benison, Jonathan. 1984. Jean Baudrillard on the Current State of SF. *Foundation* 32: 25–41.
Brown, Mick. 1993. *Cult Classics* (episode 2). BBC Radio 4, 17 October.
Bukatman, Scott. 1993. *Terminal Identity: The Virtual Subject in Postmodern Science Fiction*. Durham NC: Duke University Press.
Butler, Andrew M. 2012. *Solar Flares: Science Fiction in the 1970s*. Liverpool: Liverpool University Press.
Duffy, Christopher. 2016. Hidden Heterotopias in *Crash*. In *J.G. Ballard: Landscapes of Tomorrow*, ed. Richard Brown et al., 112–125. Leiden and Boston: Brill/Rodopi.
Durham, Scott. 1998. *Phantom Communities: The Simulacrum and the Limits of Postmodernism*. Stanford: Stanford University Press.
Eco, Umberto. 1987. *Travels in Hyperreality*. Trans. William Weaver. London: Picador.
Fisher, Mark. 2004. Why I Want to Fuck Ronald Reagan. *K-Punk*, June 13. http://k-punk.abstractdynamics.org/archives/003268.html (accessed 29/04/23).
Foster, Dennis A. 1993. J.G. Ballard's Empire of the Senses: Perversion and Failure of Authority. *PMLA* 108: 519–532.
Goddard, James, and David Pringle. 1976. An Interview with J.G. Ballard. *Vector* 73/74: 28–49.
Hayles, N. Katharine. 1991. The Borders of Madness. *Science Fiction Studies* 18 (3): 321–323.
Hultkrans, Andrew. 1997. Body Work. *Artforum* 35 (7): 76–80.
McQueen, Sean. 2011. Fearful Symmetry: Technophilia and the Science Fiction Cyborg in J.G. Ballard's and David Cronenberg's *Crash*. *Colloquy* 22: 4–23.
Murphet, Julian. 2005. Fiction and Postmodernity. In *The Cambridge History of Twentieth-Century English Literature*, ed. Laura Marcus and Peter Nicholls, 716–735. Cambridge: Cambridge University Press.
Poynor, Rick. 2004. Crash Covers. *Eye* 52. https://www.eyemagazine.com/feature/article/crash-covers (accessed 16/04/23).
Pringle, David. 1974. *Foundation* 6: 83–6.
Reynolds, Simon. 2005. *Rip It Up and Start Again: Post-punk 1978–1984*. London: Faber.
Self, Will. 1995. *Junk Mail*. London: Bloomsbury.
Sobchack, Vivian. 1991. Baudrillard's Obscenity. *Science Fiction Studies* 18 (3): 327–329.
Sontag, Susan. 1994 (1969). *Styles of Radical Will*. London: Vintage.
Sterenberg, Matthew. 2011. Mythographers of the Catastrophe: J.G. Ballard, the "New Wave", and Mythic Science Fiction. *Waseda Global Forum* 8: 257–276.

Tennant, Emma. 1999. *Burnt Diaries*. London: Canongate.
Vanhanen, Janne. 2019. The Crash-Event: Repetition and Difference in J.G. Ballard's *Crash*. *Journal of Somaesthetics* 5 (1): 61–74.
Wenaus, Andrew. 2016. The Speculative Turn and J.G. Ballard's Extro-Science Fiction. In *Deep Ends 3*, ed. Rick McGrath, 188–195. Toronto: Terminal Press.
Whiting, Emma. 2012. Disaffection and Abjection in J.G. Ballard's *The Atrocity Exhibition* and *Crash*. In *J.G. Ballard: Visions and Revisions*, ed. Jeannette Baxter and Rowland Wymer, 88–104. Basingstoke: Palgrave Macmillan.

CHAPTER 3

Writing *Crash:* Modernism/Science Fiction/*New Worlds*

Abstract This chapter argues that *Crash* should not be read as a single novel but as an event composed of multiple iterations. By regarding *Crash* as a process rather than a product, it is possible to see why the text continues to be reproduced through the work of others. The chapter reassembles the history of *Crash*'s writing, from its genesis in Ballard's *The Atrocity Exhibition* to its staging as an art installation, a proposed performance piece, and a drama-documentary. This narrative, though, is also entangled in the increasingly fraught history of *New Worlds* magazine, and in the relationship between science fiction, the counterculture and the avant-garde of the late 1960s.

Keywords New Wave • Alfred Jarry • Wyndham Lewis • Technology • Multi-media

By the time that Ballard submitted the manuscript of *Crash* in February 1972, he was emotionally exhausted. The task of thinking himself into the perverse logic of Vaughan and his willing accomplice, the narrator and Ballard's namesake, had caused him profound psychological distress. Speaking in 1974, Ballard commented that *Crash* was a 'deranging book to write':

© The Author(s), under exclusive license to Springer Nature Switzerland AG 2025
P. March-Russell, *J. G. Ballard's* Crash, Palgrave Science Fiction and Fantasy: A New Canon,
https://doi.org/10.1007/978-3-031-73094-8_3

Such an extreme metaphor ... the effort of maintaining the logic of 2 plus 2 equals 5 or minus 7, or 99, anything but 4. I sort of hated myself as I wrote the book because I felt I was dealing in ... deadly things, like a sort of arms salesman. Much of the book was morally highly objectionable, there's no doubt about that. (*IT* 22)

The equation that underwrote the novel consisted of two halves. On the one side, an examination of the 'logic' that permits hundreds of thousands of car-related deaths per year: '*Millions* are injured, and seriously too' (23). On the other side, an investigation into a perverse yet utopian desire: 'A new Krafft-Ebing is being written by car crashes, televised violence, modern architecture and design. ... I can see a sexual experience of extraordinary complexity, beauty, tenderness, and love. I can see the magic of sex on a planetary scale, revivifying everything it touches' (Tarshis 1973). How Ballard arrived at this formula, neatly summarised as 'sex times technology equals the future' (*EM* 54), is the subject of this chapter. *Crash*, in all of its unruliness, was the result of a process that took nearly a decade, reiterated through multi-media experiments, as well as Ballard's participation in *New Worlds* magazine's attempt to modernise science fiction. Due to its compositional history, *Crash* should be regarded less as a novel and more as an event, 'insofar as it refuses to be absorbed into the *order* of a classical narrative, brought to book in a narrative *account*, its tension exchanged for other tensions' (Bennington 1988, 109). This lack of closure means that the text continues to be written through seemingly endless adaptation and reproduction in contemporary culture.

In May 1964, Michael Moorcock assumed the editorship of *New Worlds*, the premier British SF magazine. Although it would take him another three years to transform *New Worlds* into an avant-garde title, Moorcock began publishing the work of more artistically ambitious authors as well as a series of combative editorials and features. His first issue in charge not only demanded 'a new literature for the Space Age' to formally represent 'our ad-saturated, Bomb-dominated, power-corrupted times' (Moorcock 2010, 364), but also featured Ballard's appreciation of William Burroughs, whose collage novels indicated that SF had exhausted its 'conventions', 'assumptions' and 'repertory of ideas' with which to depict 'the age of Cape Canaveral, Hiroshima and Belsen' (*UG* 129–30). Two issues earlier, Ballard had published the first of his experimental stories, 'The Terminal Beach' (1964), which described the labyrinthine structure of an abandoned nuclear test-site in blocks of data that included sub-sections, interpolated documents and a non-linear chronology. Two years later, Ballard published the first four of his *Atrocity Exhibition* texts that condensed narrative even further so that, as he commented at the time, the realms of public, private and psychological space collapse:

> On one level, the world of public events, Cape Kennedy and Viet Nam mimetised on billboards. On another level, the immediate personal environment, the volumes of space enclosed by my opposed hands, the geometry of my own postures, the time-values contained in this room, the motion-space of highways, staircases, the angles between these walls. On a third level, the inner world of the psyche. Where these planes intersect, images are born. With these co-ordinates, some kind of valid reality begins to clarify itself. (*SN* 8)

Although *Crash* returned to a more linear construction, Ballard confirmed that it relied 'equally on this technique' (*EM* 74). For Moorcock (2010, 379), Ballard's innovations amounted to 'the first clear voice of a movement destined to consolidate the literary ideas ... of the twentieth century, forming them into ... a new instrument for dealing with the world of the future contained, observable, in the world of the present'. Six issues after this editorial, in July 1967, Moorcock published the first large-size format of *New Worlds*, thereby consolidating the work of writers and artists for whom Ballard was an avatar. The magazine would now become what Moorcock (1983, 11) had envisaged in 1964: decorated with 'good quality illustrations' and specialising 'in experimental work by writers like Burroughs and artists like Paolozzi', 'a cross-fertilization of popular sf, science and the work of the literary and artistic avant-garde'.

If, however, Moorcock saw *New Worlds* as a synthesis between speculative fiction, scientific ideas and modernist techniques, then Ballard was hatching something altogether more disruptive. In his analysis of *Crash*'s opening chapter, Mike Holliday has isolated the novel's key motifs: the car, death, celebrity, sex, surveillance, abstraction, corporeality, disaffection, psychopathy and rebirth. He then details how these themes gradually emerged in Ballard's fiction before coalescing around the figure of the car crash in 'Notes Towards a Mental Breakdown', originally published as 'The Death Module' in that same, pivotal July 1967 issue of *New Worlds*.

A crucial catalyst, though, was the sudden death of Ballard's wife, Mary, whilst on holiday in September 1964: 'After watching her being buried in the cemetery at Alicante, Ballard drove his three young children all the way back to England: another long, desperate car journey' (Holliday 2017). For the next eighteen months, Ballard produced little until the first of the *Atrocity Exhibition* stories, 'You and Me and the Continuum', in March 1966. If, on the one hand, Ballard was in a state of shock after Mary's death, whilst at the same time adjusting to the demands of single parenthood, then on the other hand, he was transposing his trauma onto what he was witnessing via the TV screen: the assassination of John F. Kennedy and the suicide of Marilyn Monroe; race riots and the escalation of the Vietnam War; the Moor Murderers and the commodification of violence in popular drama. Ballard became fascinated by films of test car collisions, which the safety campaigner Ralph Nader also used as part of his research for the best-selling *Unsafe at Any Speed* (1965):

> It was like some strange technological ballet. I remember looking at these films and thinking about the strange psychological dimensions they seemed to touch. They seemed to say something about the way everything becomes more and more stylised, more and more cut off from ordinary feeling. (Cokeliss 1971)

In 'Notes Towards a Mental Breakdown', though, the neutral description of crash test dummies in 'You and Me and the Continuum' is replaced by the immersive attempt of the protagonist (here known as Trabert) to restage Kennedy's death as a car crash:

> These erotic films, over which presided the mutilated figure of Ralph Nader, were screened above Dr Nathan's head as he moved along the lines of crashed cars. ... During the interval when the reels changed, Dr Nathan noticed that Trabert was peering at the photographs pinned to the windshields of the crashed cars. From the balcony of his empty office Catherine Austin watched him with barely focused eyes. Her leg stance, significant indicator of sexual arousal, confirmed all Dr Nathan had anticipated of Trabert's involvement with the events of Dealey Plaza. (*AE* 46)

For Trabert, the car crash represents 'a disaster in space' (48) that forcibly merges the public, private and psychological realms. Although each plane is fictional in itself, since each fabricates a version of reality, their sudden collision compels a new kind of reality to emerge, one closer to what the psychoanalyst Jacques Lacan terms 'the Real'. The irony, though, is that to see this, the reader must adopt Trabert's paranoid vision whilst, at the same time, Ballard fictionalises his theory of intersecting planes by voicing it, almost verbatim, through Dr Nathan (51).

Having now harnessed the key themes that would become *Crash*, Ballard proceeded to refine them in the subsequent *Atrocity Exhibition* stories. As Samuel Francis (2011, 111–12) has argued, the repetitions, re-enactments and substitutions that structure *Crash*'s narrative take their cue from Sigmund Freud's essay, 'Beyond the Pleasure Principle' (1920), but this pattern is also evident in how Ballard researched and rehearsed the ideas that would become the novel. These reiterations are embedded in the story, 'The University of Death' (1968), in which the protagonist (now known as Talbot) persuades a group of students into staging a 'Festival of Atrocity Films' as part of his own 'calculated psycho-drama' (*AE* 14–15). One of the students, Koester, becomes obsessed with Talbot, organises an 'exhibition of crashed cars' and produces 'a magazine devoted solely to car accidents: *Crash!*' (21). Ballard's fictionalisation of his own multi-media experiments suggests a kind of metatextuality often associated with the playfulness of postmodernism (Waugh 1984). Ballard, however, offers a more radical critique by regarding the very act of writing as a site where public, private and psychological planes intersect. The constant networking of data from these sources means that the page, let alone the individual sentence, becomes overloaded; the original magazine publications of stories such as 'Plan for the Assassination of Jacqueline Kennedy' (1967) and 'The Summer Cannibals' (1969) were heavily illustrated with images that distract the reader's attention. For Rob Latham (2011, 289), the 'collage techniques' pioneered in *New Worlds* 'held up to postwar culture a series of distorting mirrors, reflecting back its incipient rage and anomie.' Such a political reading is, however, unclear in Ballard's work since it implies an instrumentality that his writing actively resists. Instead, as Ballard proposes:

> We live in a world ruled by fictions of every kind – mass merchandising, advertising, politics conducted as a branch of advertising, the instant translation of science and technology into popular imagery, the increasing blurring and intermingling of identities within the realm of consumer goods, the preempting of any free or imaginative response to experience by the television screen. We live inside an enormous novel. (*C* 4–5)

If public, private and psychological life is exclusively a fantasy, and the only way a writer can 'invent the reality' (5) is to violently collide them, then what both *The Atrocity Exhibition* and *Crash* represent is not the looking-glass world of postmodernism but the pataphysics of Alfred Jarry, the Symbolist writer to whom Ballard was especially indebted for *The Atrocity Exhibition*'s closing chapter, 'The Assassination of John Fitzgerald Kennedy Considered as a Downhill Motor Race' (1966).[1]

Jarry's ideas were of especial importance to *New Worlds*. Moorcock had cited him in his second editorial in 1964 while the concept of the multiverse, already introduced in Moorcock's *The Sundered Worlds* (1962) and soon to become integral to the Jerry Cornelius stories, was a variant of Jarry's '*virtualité*'. In his posthumous novel, *Exploits & Opinions of Dr Faustroll, Pataphysician* (1911), Jarry's hero escapes imprisonment by transcending to a higher dimension, visualised in the text as an ocean, dotted with islands, which flows through the streets of Paris. Faustroll's method of escape is pataphysics, defined by Jarry (1996, 21–2) as 'the science of imaginary solutions' whose aim is to 'examine the laws governing exceptions' and 'explain the universe supplementary to this one'. One of the intellectual roots of pataphysics was the philosophy of Friedrich Nietzsche (1998, 359), in particular, his claim that 'truths are illusions of which one has forgotten that they *are* illusions; worn-out metaphors which have become powerless to affect the senses'. To lie is to therefore uphold the logic of truth, as it has been instrumentalised by reason and social convention, 'to form exact classifications, and never to violate the order of castes and the sequences of rank' (360). To be truthful, to be authentic in an inauthentic world, is to not only recognise the metaphoricity of truth but to also reclaim oneself as an imaginative, ludic and, above all, '*artistically creating* subject' (361). Such a sentiment not only appealed to Jarry's primacy upon the human imagination but also his sense that reality is the 'exception' that art must 'supplement'. Ballard too makes reference to Nietzsche, specifically his distinction of Apollonian reason that screens out Dionysiac desires of sex and horror: 'if anything is to have meaning for us it must take place in terms of the values and experiences of the media landscape … this sort of Dionysiac landscape of the 1970s' (*EM* 33).

Yet Jarry's novel, although playful, is written with a quasi-scientific detachment, and he not only prides himself in embedding his more fantastical claims in real-world science but also actively incorporates scientists such as C.V. Boys, William Crookes and Lord Kelvin within the pataphysical spaces explored by Faustroll. Like *The Atrocity Exhibition*, there is (in Ballard's words) a 'blurring and intermingling' of the real with the virtual that exposes the extent to which reality has already been fictionalised. Following Jarry's lead, Ballard extends this principle to include his own experiences and compositional method—nothing lies outside what, for Ballard, is already a pataphysical life lived out in the all-consuming spectacle of the media landscape. The clearest example of this in *The Atrocity Exhibition* are the mock scientific reports that pastiche behavioural studies as a provider of fiction about the unconscious desires of their test subjects. But the last, entitled 'Crash!' (1969), is also notable for providing a set of conclusions that seed the next stage of Ballard's research project:

> The twentieth century has also given birth to a vast range of machines – computers, pilotless planes, thermonuclear weapons – where the latent identity of the machine is ambiguous ... An understanding of this identity can be found in a study of the automobile, which dominates the vectors of speed, aggression, violence and desire. In particular the automobile crash contains a crucial image of the machine as conceptualized psychopathology. ... It is clear that the car crash is seen as a fertilizing rather than a destructive experience, a liberation of sexual and machine libido, mediating the sexuality of those who have died with an erotic intensity impossible in any other form. (*AE* 111–12).

As Ballard repeatedly remarked, it is 'the *idea* of the car crash that is sexually exciting – not the crash itself', since it draws upon 'all kinds of unconscious fantasies – of transcendence, of death' (Hultkrans 1997, 80). Ballard went further still, arguing that 'I'm not interested in cars themselves. It's technology that interests me' (Anon 2013, 26), and that 'it's not the car that's important: it's *driving*':

> One spends a substantial part of one's life in the motor car and the experience of driving condenses many of the experiences of being a human being in 1970, the marriage of physical aspects of ourselves with the imaginative and technological aspects of our lives. I think the twentieth century reaches just about its highest expression on the highway. Everything is there, the speed and violence of our age, its love of stylisation, fashion, the organisational side of things – what I call the elaborately signalled landscape. (*EM* 31)

This quotation, in revised form, recurs in Harley Cokeliss's film *Crash!* (1971) that ends with Ballard looking down from the parapet of a multi-storey car park and intoning: 'modern technology is beginning to reach into our dreams and change our whole way of looking at things and perceiving reality ... more and more it is drawing us away from contemplating ourselves to contemplating *its* world' (Cokeliss 1971).

Ballard's depiction of a technological sensorium complemented critics, such as Jacques Ellul, and media theorists, most notably Marshall McLuhan, whose representation of consumer culture as a high-speed information mosaic Ballard would often invoke. But it also complements critics of mass culture, such as Susan Sontag (2001, 13), for whom 'Ours is a culture based on excess, on overproduction; the result is a steady loss of sharpness in our sensory experience. All the conditions of modern life – its material plenitude, its sheer crowdedness – conjoin to dull our sensory faculties'. However, whereas Sontag's response is an 'erotics of art' (14) based upon a renewed sensory awareness, Ballard's reaction is to give himself over to this alien technology that he anthropomorphises as sentient and libidinous. Although hardly a Marxist, Ballard nonetheless evokes Karl Marx's (1976, 163) fantastical description of commodity fetishism:

> The form of wood, for instance, is altered if a table is made out of it. Nevertheless the table continues to be wood, an ordinary, sensuous thing. But as it soon as it emerges as a commodity, it changes into a thing which transcends sensuousness. It not only stands with its feet on the ground, but, in relation to all other commodities, it stands on its head, and evolves out of its wooden brain grotesque ideas.

Like Freud's distinction between the manifest and latent content of the dream-work, there is a disparity between what the commodity is and what it signifies; a phantasmal existence that, like Jarry's Faustroll, Ballard seeks to explore and inhabit: 'you don't buy an airline ticket just to take you from London to New York any more—what you're buying is an image of a certain kind of transportation style. The food, the in-flight movies, the stewardesses' uniforms, all contribute to a fiction designed to serve an imaginative aim' (*IT* 20).

Although there are similarities here with Roland Barthes's notion of 'mythologies' or Jean Baudrillard's early work *The System of Objects* (1968), Ballard's emphasis upon the technical organisation of this late capitalist dreamworld is indebted to an early influence both upon himself and McLuhan: the arch modernist and satirist Wyndham Lewis.[2] Writing in the aftermath of World War I, Lewis (1969, 253) argued that the forces of economic and technological modernity conspired to erect a 'screen' between reality and humanity:

The 'dark night of the soul' into which the individual is relapsing, the intellectual shoddiness of so much of the thought responsible for the artist's reality, or 'nature', today, all these things seem to point to the desirability for a new, and if necessary, shattering criticism of 'modernity'.

The retreat of Lewis's contemporaries, such as James Joyce and Gertrude Stein, into subjective expression amounts to a kind of infantilism: it fails to comprehend the ideological veil by which capitalist oppression of the subject sustains itself. What the Romantic writer perceives as a 'dark night of the soul' is, by contrast, the union of economic, technological and bureaucratic forces that render the subject 'powerless, unsatisfying, circumscribed' (250–1). Instead, what passes for human is no more than a performance: 'all men are necessarily comic: for they are all *things*, or physical bodies, behaving as *persons*' (Lewis 2004, 158). Since, in Lewis's model, subjectivity has already been liquidated, humans have already become cyborgs and can be controlled like machines:

> By his education he has been made into an ingeniously free-looking, easy-moving, 'civilized', gentlemanly Robot. At a word ..., at the pressing of a button, all of these hallucinated automata, with their technician-trained minds and bodies, can be released against each other. (Lewis 1926, 111–12).

It is but a short step from Lewis's machine-men to Burroughs's (2010, 79) Nova Police with 'antennae ears tuned to all voices of the city ... green disc eyes covered with pupils of a pale electric blue', or to Ballard's vision of the car becoming an 'organo-metal structure' with 'half-conscious identifications between machine and body' (Anon 2013, 36). With his hallucinatory landscapes and preoccupation with control systems, Burroughs's fiction represents a midpoint between Jarry and Lewis. Although other members of the twentieth-century avant-garde, most notably, Jean Genet, Franz Kafka, F.T. Marinetti and Raymond Roussel, contribute to the genesis of *Crash*, these three writers form a significant triad for understanding Ballard's inspiration.

Ballard's last set of influences was more immediate and personal. The story 'Crash!' had been published as part of an ICA (Institute for Contemporary Arts) newsletter, a remnant of an unrealised project with Ballard's friend, the computer scientist Christopher Evans. As Ballard later acknowledged, after a lengthy mourning for Mary, there 'came a ... desperate promiscuity, a form of shock treatment' (*ML* 204) to revive himself.

Nonetheless, he remained haunted by the feeling that 'nature had committed a dreadful crime' against his wife and family (205), a grief possibly exacerbated by his wartime experiences of invasion, death, destruction, internment and migration: 'the sense that reality itself was a stage set that could be dismantled at any moment' (58). Despite living on the edges of London, and caring for his young children, Ballard now became relatively gregarious, thanks to Moorcock and his then wife and *New Worlds* collaborator Hilary Bailey, who were living in fashionable Ladbroke Grove. Ballard had already met Martin Bax, paediatrician and editor of the literary magazine *Ambit*, in 1965 and he was friends with the poet and radio presenter George MacBeth; both *Ambit* and the BBC's Third Programme became important platforms for Ballard to experiment with multi-media forms and disseminate his ideas further. But, in the space of six weeks in 1967, Moorcock introduced Ballard to three life-changing people: Evans, the artist Eduardo Paolozzi, and Ballard's future partner Claire Walsh. The sudden acceleration in Ballard's social life seemed to complement the dizzying speed of public events responded to in *The Atrocity Exhibition*.

Evans, like Ballard, was fascinated by impending technological changes, especially in terms of mass communications. The two formed a close bond, collaborating on computer-generated poems for *Ambit*, exchanging scientific research papers, and touring breakers' yards for crashed cars. Evans became the physical template for Vaughan, the rogue scientist in *Crash*, who made his first appearance in the last of the *Atrocity Exhibition* stories to be published, 'Tolerances of the Human Face' (1969). The title itself had been suggested by Walsh who, through her job in publishing, had discovered a study with the Ballardian heading, 'Tolerances of the Human Face in Crash Impacts'. Studies such as these, and in particular Jacob Kulowski's medical textbook *Crash Injuries* (1960), became vital sources for Ballard. Walsh herself became the reluctant subject of two of Ballard's mock advertisements published in *Ambit*, which reworked language and themes from *The Atrocity Exhibition* (Poynor 2014); when Ballard wanted to use Claire as the name of James's wife in *Crash*, Walsh objected. As Ballard later admitted, the fictional marriage of James and Catherine mirrored the strained relations between Ballard and Walsh as he wrote the novel (Coillard 1998), which would result in a five-year separation. Lastly, Paolozzi had an anonymous cameo appearance in *Crash* as James's 'close friend' who visits the Imperial War Museum with him, and experiences 'the pathos that surrounded the cockpit segment of a World War II Japanese Zero fighter aircraft' (*C* 68).

Ballard not only fictionalised his closest companions but, in 'Tolerances of the Human Face', also recounted for the first time his departure from the internment camp at Lunghua, articulating it through his protagonist (here called Travers) in a parody of Ernest Hemingway's prose style. The borderlines between history, memory and fiction become increasingly porous, subject to the desensitising effects of what Ballard now called 'the death of affect', so that it is no coincidence that its description from the French introduction to *Crash* is rehearsed here, almost verbatim, by Dr Nathan:

> Consider our most real and tender pleasures – in the excitement of pain and mutilation; in sex as the perfect arena, like a culture-bed of sterile pus, for all the veronicas of our own perversions, in voyeurism and self-disgust, in our moral freedom to pursue our own psychopathologies as a game, and in our ever greater powers for abstraction. (*AE* 84)

It is also no surprise that there is passing reference to 'a stage show, entitled "Crash"' (86). In April 1968, Ballard submitted a synopsis for a 'science theatre presentation' to the ICA (Beckett 2019). Mike Kustow, its new Director, had a background in radical theatre, most notably, with the Royal Shakespeare Company's production of Peter Brooks's innovative, anti-Vietnam War play *US* (1966). Kustow was open to new ideas in thinking about the future: in May 1968 he attended the Brighton Festival, where the central theme was science fiction, and met, amongst others, Ballard, Moorcock and Brian Aldiss. In August, the exhibition *Cybernetic Serendipity* opened at the ICA, showcasing computer-related art, film, literature and music from the likes of Bruce Lacey, Gustav Metzger, Nam June Paik and Peter Zinovieff. The ICA, under Kustow's leadership, was therefore a suitable venue for Ballard's proposal. Yet despite advance publicity in the *Sunday Mirror* (19 May), under the attention-grabbing headline 'A Star Role for the Beloved Monster that Lives on Sex and Sacrifice', the show was not staged. Since Ballard continued to work with the ICA, most notably in the 1972 *Ambit* event where the striptease artist, Euphoria Bliss, performed her reading of a scientific paper, 'The Side-Effects of Orthonovin G', it is most likely that the show was cancelled due to other projects.

Tonally, however, the synopsis tends towards the didactic. Centre-stage is 'the beloved monster', a crashed car. The characters consist of a nuclear family (mother, father, son), the boy's fiancée, and a salesman. A lecturer, played by Evans, delivers reports and statistics about the design and safety of cars. The cast, as if emerging from an Absurdist drama such as Eugène Ionesco's *The Bald Prima Donna* (1950), parrot the clichés of advertising and sales brochures. The family are persuaded into buying the car for the young couple despite ominous voice-overs that refer to crash injuries and a background film that alternates between idealised images of car ownership and violent accidents. In the second section, the couple begin to make love in (and to) the car; a design stylist indicates the car's in-built sexual geometry; and the backdrop images, first erotic, are replaced by footage of multiple collisions. The actors stare at this imagery in awed fascination; the lecturer reveals that, despite all the safety propaganda, car design enables this deathly desire. From then on, the parents and the fiancée conspire in planning the optimum car death for the son: a sacrificial victim in a highly stylised and ritualised performance. Despite elements that appear in the novel, what Ballard possibly learnt most from the synopsis—and why it might not have been performed—was that agit-prop was not the right tone for this narrative. Instead, it needed to be more immersive, enthralling and ambiguous; effects that Ballard achieved during the rigorous editing of the manuscript in 1972.

There were, however, two further iterations as Ballard worked on the first draft. In April 1970, he staged his 'Crashed Cars' exhibition at the New Arts Lab, Camden. Also known as the Institute for Research in Arts and Technology, the New Arts Lab had opened in October 1969, consisting of a faction that had split off from the soon-to-be defunct Drury Arts Lab with artists such as John (Hoppy) Hopkins, Malcolm Le Grice, John Lifton and Pamela Zoline (Curtis 2020, 91). Lifton had exhibited at the ICA's *Cybernetic Serendipity* whilst both he and Le Grice were members of the Computer Arts Society that held its inaugural exhibition at the Royal College of Art in March 1969. Hopkins was an advocate of video art and grassroots TV and was in correspondence with the then Minister of Technology, Tony Benn, thereby capitalising on the Labour Government's rhetoric around the 'white heat' of technological change (92). Zoline, who had studied with the Pop Artists Claes Oldenburg and Roy Lichtenstein, was friends with her fellow US expatriates and *New Worlds* writers, Thomas M. Disch and John Sladek. Through their encouragement, she composed the quintessential *New Worlds* story, 'The Heat Death of the Universe' (1967), and also contributed significantly to the look and design of the magazine (Dillon 2020, 218–61). Besides exhibiting her own work at the New Arts Lab, Zoline ran the gallery and commissioned Ballard's piece. Ballard, like Evans, was also a trustee of the New Arts Lab (Curtis 2020, 121).

The exhibition consisted of three crashed cars: a Pontiac, typifying Ballard's observation 'that the future is something with a fin on it' (Cokeliss 1971); a Mini, identified with sporty 60s culture, thanks in part to the recent heist movie *The Italian Job* (1969); and its antithesis, the soberly conservative Austin Cambridge A60. All, as Simon Ford (2005) observes, 'were now in a sense equivalent; smashed and levelled to the raw material of their crushed metal, broken glass, and stained upholstery'. They were displayed with no explanation apart from a handout that adapted the relevant passage from the short story 'Crash!' and an opening statement that suggested each car was 'a memorial to a unique collision between man and his technology. ... Behind our horror lie an undeniable fascination and excitement, most clearly revealed by the deaths of the famous: Jayne Mansfield and James Dean, Albert Camus and John F. Kennedy' (quoted Ford 2005). Ballard claimed that he had employed a close-circuit TV to monitor the reactions of the visitors and a semi-naked woman, Jo Stanley, to interview them. In Ballard's 1971 account, the event degenerated into a Bacchanalian feast:

> I'd never seen 100 people get drunk so quickly. ... Wine was poured over the crashed cars, glasses were broken, the topless girl was nearly raped in the back seat of the Pontiac by some self-aggrandising character. The show went on for a month. In that time they came up against massive hostility... The cars were attacked, windows ripped off. (*EM* 40)

Ballard subsequently claimed that the party became 'a drunken brawl' which acted 'as a green light' (*SN* 318) for starting *Crash*, although in fact he had already begun writing it. Talking about the event in 1982, however, Ballard makes no mention of the opening night's violence: the visitors instead reacted with 'shock and nervous laughter'. He refers to people returning 'to attack the cars and destroy them further' (*EM* 143) although doubt has been cast upon that (Curtis 2020, 117). Stanley herself denied the attempted assault and wrote a negative review in the underground magazine *Friends* (29 May 1970); more recently, she has called the show 'a dismal non-event' (Sweet 2023).

In 1991, Ballard fictionalised his memories of the exhibition in *The Kindness of Women*. Ballard's alter-ego displays a trio of crashed cars that explore the 'acts of numbing brutality' which leach 'away all feeling and emotion' in 'an ecology of violence' (*KW* 221). What is notable about this sequence is the extent to which Ballard reworks imagery from *Crash*, extracts its French introduction for the fictional catalogue, and lifts phrases and whole sentences from both *The Atrocity Exhibition* and his interviews about the show. Later still, in his memoir, Ballard reiterates phrases almost verbatim from *The Kindness of Women* and his earlier recollections (*ML* 238–40), so that the historical event is thoroughly blurred between its remembrance and its fictionalisation. The point here is that, although Ballard's recollection has been contested by other witnesses, it is not a case of saying whether Ballard is lying or not; rather, the exhibition has been subsumed into Ballard's pataphysical retelling of his own life-story and of *Crash*'s creation.

This dreamscape is powerfully reinforced in Cokeliss's collaboration with Ballard for the BBC2 arts strand, *Review*, in February 1971. The short film features Ballard both as himself and as a version of the protean protagonist in *The Atrocity Exhibition*. In addition to Ballard's voice-over, reiterating ideas now commonplace from his fiction, reviews and interviews, spoken readings occur in which the actress Gabrielle Drake appears as a version of Karen Novotny, the woman who is repeatedly killed by Ballard's anti-hero. Drake is presented as a spectre, abruptly appearing and disappearing, often filmed in slow-motion or in time-lapse, static with a vacant or inert stare. She is silent yet narrated in the readings; viewed alternately in extreme close-up, as a series of body parts (hands, shoulders, back, breasts, thighs, legs), or in the middle distance as an isolated standing object. But although Drake's character appears to be subaltern—an object without subjectivity defined solely within the gaze of either Ballard's persona or Cokeliss's camera—her random appearances seem to come unheeded from the male unconscious, that is, the points at which the planes of public, private and psychological space intersect. According to Ballard's own theory, Drake's character may be the only real figure in Cokeliss's film whereas Ballard's persona as the obsessive, compulsive writer is no less a fiction than the showroom, carwash, carpark and highway that he inhabits. At the very end, Drake turns her back on Ballard's gaze and walks out of camera shot into the technological landscape, a sign not only of agency but also, in a characteristic move in Ballard's fiction, 'of psychological fulfilment', where the self merges 'in the ultimate metaphor, the ultimate image' (*DM* 91). Filmed whilst Ballard was revising the first draft of *Crash*, Drake's characterisation may have fed significantly into how the novel's women are portrayed, not least the naming of the disabled character Gabrielle.

For the next year, then, Ballard was immersed in the rewriting of *Crash* even as his personal and financial difficulties mounted. *New Worlds* meanwhile had closed as a monthly magazine in October 1970, to be reborn as a quarterly, kept afloat by Moorcock's own frantic writing. The New Wave was rapidly disintegrating and relations between the principal players were becoming frayed. Speaking in November 1970, Ballard expressed dismay that *New Worlds* had 'ceased to be a science fiction magazine' and, whilst exempting Moorcock, argued that 'The writers are to blame' since 'Without a good or original idea no amount of experimental technique can produce anything of interest' (Goddard 2013, 30). Ballard later elaborated that 'writers like Sladek, Disch, Spinrad, Pam Zoline, Mike Moorcock himself, none of these are really science fiction writers in the sense that I am a science fiction writer' (Goddard and Pringle 1976, 43). Although, by his own admission, Ballard only used the surface trappings of SF to explore a more surreal, psychological terrain, he continued to privilege his origins, alongside Aldiss, within the pages of genre titles such as *New Worlds* and *Science Fantasy* (*SN* 334). At the time of writing *Crash*, Ballard routinely staged vigorous defences of SF as the most 'important fiction being written now' since 'our lives are being invaded by science, technology and their applications' (*EM* 23). By contrast, first in his essay 'The Innocent as Paranoid' (1969), and then in the French introduction to *Crash*, Ballard discounted literary modernism as solipsistic and anachronistic, wedded to 'the monolithic character of Victorianism and the tyranny of the paterfamilias': 'if anything befits the 20th century it is optimism, the iconography of mass merchandising, naivety and a guilt-free enjoyment of all the mind's possibilities' (*C* 2). Yet, Ballard's characterisation of modernism was as selective as his putative genealogy of science fiction, from H.G. Wells to Burroughs and Paolozzi via Aldous Huxley and Bernard Wolfe. Ballard, however, was equally influenced by such modernists as Jarry and Lewis. His critique then resembles the kind of *détournement* witnessed in his fiction: a hijacking and re-routing of both modernism and science fiction in order to generate a space outside of both canonical literature and standard genre history.

Ballard's final statement on the writing of *Crash* was precipitated by Peter Nicholls's jeremiad in the journal *Foundation* against the New Wave, accusing it of nihilism, hedonism and cynicism. Ballard was his principal target and *Crash* his prize exhibit. Nicholls (1975, 31) wrote of Ballard's moral vacuity: 'minglings of flesh and technology, advertising and death ... are accepted and welcomed by him with a placid, Buddha-like smile'. Although Aldiss and Moorcock leapt to Ballard's defence, they did so from their own entrenched positions: Aldiss seeking to recuperate Ballard's work within his own history of SF recently detailed in *Billion Year Spree* (1973) and Moorcock actively disdainful of the SF genre. Ballard's response was both the most instructive and the least helpful: '*Crash* ... is an example of a kind of terminal irony, where not even the writer knows where he stands' (*TL* 51). Although 'terminal irony' has been compared with Baudrillard's evasive 'fatal strategy' (Luckhurst 2005, 516), a more accurate comparison is with Lewis's 'moronic inferno' (1984, 183), in which the author descends into the unredeemed hell of human folly, his own included. The abdication of authorial responsibility, moreover, echoes the very origins of modernist prose in the composition of Gustave Flaubert's *Madame Bovary* (1857):

> You can have no idea of the kind of book I am writing. In my other books I was slovenly; in this I am trying to be impeccable and to follow a geometrically straight line. No lyricism, no comments, the author's personality absent. It will make dreary reading; it will contain atrocious things of misery and sordidness. (Flaubert 1963, 90–1)

Ballard, too, saw *Crash* as a break with his previous novels as he sought to be 'free of any sf overtones' (*CC*, 7 April 1972). Whilst still engaged in writing a 'landscape of the future', Ballard not only returned to a linear form and removed all element of himself apart from his name, he also produced a novel that featured 'long passages of boredom', a 'grim logic' and a 'sexual experience that we secretly desire' (*CC*, 10 April 1972). Ballard vacillated at what he had written, describing it variously as 'a science fiction of the present' (*EM* 125), 'not a science fiction novel, but could nevertheless be read as one' (*EM* 73) or a form of technological fiction (*RS* 32). Only after the success of *Empire of the Sun* (1984), and the emergence of a new hard SF in the form of cyberpunk, did Ballard cement his now retrospective view of *Crash* as being in no way science fiction.

In 1973, however, when *Crash* finally materialised, it defied all generic expectations. This was a book as total object and, as such, a surreal artefact. To understand how Ballard's satirical aims intermeshed with his novel's surrealism, we must now explore his friendship with Paolozzi, the role of Pop Art, and the debt to surrealism's anthropological investigations.

Notes

1. Florian Cord (2017) has also noted Jarry's importance for Ballard but reads pataphysics solely through Baudrillard's appropriation of the concept, in which it is instrumentalised as a variant of the 'fatal strategy'. Cord's overestimation of Ballard as a critic of late capitalism, effectively looking backwards from such novels as *Kingdom Come* (2006), is counteracted by Duncan Bell's (2021) reading of Ballard's liberal beliefs.
2. Ballard acknowledged in 1956 that the three writers who interested him most were Edgar Allan Poe, Wyndham Lewis and Bernard Wolfe (*FSS* 15). Besides Ballard's essay on Lewis, 'Visions of Hell' (1966), Moorcock reprinted Lewis's artwork in *New Worlds*.

Works Cited

Anon. 2013 (1975). The *Repsychling* Interview. In *The J.G. Ballard Book*, ed. Rick McGrath, 32–9. Toronto: Terminal Press.
Beckett, Chris. 2019. J.G. Ballard's "Crash! A Science Theatre Presentation for the ICA": The Context of a Document Newly Discovered. *Electronic British Library Journal*. http://www.bl.uk/eblj/2019articles/pdf/ebljarticle82019.pdf (accessed 20/02/24).
Bell, Duncan. 2021. J.G. Ballard's Surrealist Liberalism. *Political Theory* 49 (6): 934–967.
Bennington, Geoffrey. 1988. *Lyotard: Writing the Event*. Manchester: Manchester University Press.
Burroughs, William. 2010 (1962). *The Ticket That Exploded*. London: Fourth Estate.
Coillard, Jean-Paul. 1998. J.G. Ballard: Theatre of Cruelty. *Disturb Ezine*. https://www.jgballard.ca/media/1998_disturb_magazine.html (accessed 19/02/24).
Cokeliss, Harley, dir. 1971. *Crash!* BBC2, 12 February. https://www.youtube.com/watch?v=JinzENZA90s (accessed 19/04/23).
Cord, Florian. 2017. *J.G. Ballard's Politics: Late Capitalism, Power, and the Pataphysics of Resistance*. Berlin: De Gruyter.
Curtis, David. 2020. *London's Arts Labs and the 60s Avant-Garde*. New Barnet: John Libbey Publishing.

Dillon, Tom. 2020. *'What is the Exact Nature of the Catastrophe?' A Cultural History of New Worlds Magazine, 1964–70.* Unpublished PhD dissertation. Birkbeck College, London.

Flaubert, Gustave. 1963. On Realism. In *Documents of Modern Literary Realism*, ed. George J. Becker, 89–96. Princeton: Princeton University Press.

Ford, Simon. 2005. A Psychopathic Hymn: J.G. Ballard's "Crashed Cars" Exhibition of 1970. http://www.slashseconds.org/issues/001/001/articles/13_sford/index.php (accessed 26/07/21).

Francis, Samuel. 2011. *The Psychological Fictions of J.G. Ballard.* London: Continuum.

Goddard, James. 2013 (1970). Everything is Science Fiction!. In *The J.G. Ballard Book*, ed. Rick McGrath, 16–31. Toronto: Terminal Press.

Goddard, James, and David Pringle. 1976. An Interview with J.G. Ballard. *Vector* 73/74: 28–49.

Holliday, Mike. 2017. Taking the Top Off His Skull: The Genesis of J.G. Ballard's *Crash*. https://www.holli.co.uk/crash.htm (accessed 15/02/24).

Hultkrans, Andrew. 1997. Body Work. *Artforum* 35 (7): 76–80; 117.

Jarry, Alfred. 1996 (1911). *Exploits & Opinions of Dr Faustroll, Pataphysician* Ed. and trans. Simon Watson Taylor. Boston MA: Exact Change.

Latham, Rob. 2011. Assassination Weapons: The Visual Culture of New Wave Science Fiction. In *Cutting Across Media: Appropriation Art, Interventionist Collage, and Copyright Law*, ed. Kembrew McLeod and Rudolf Kuenzli, 276–289. Durham NC: Duke University Press.

Lewis, Wyndham. 1926. *The Art of Being Ruled.* London: Chatto & Windus.

———. 1969. *Wyndham Lewis on Art: Collected Writings, 1913–1956.* Eds. Walter Michel and C.J. Fox. London: Thames and Hudson.

———. 1984 (1950). *Rude Assignment: An Intellectual Autobiography.* Ed. Toby Foshay. Santa Barbara: Black Sparrow Press.

———. 2004 (1927). *The Wild Body.* London: Penguin.

Luckhurst, Roger. 2005. J.G. Ballard: *Crash*. In *A Companion to Science Fiction*, ed. David Seed, 512–521. Oxford: Blackwell.

Marx, Karl. 1976 (1871). *Capital, vol. 1.* Trans. Ben Fowkes. Harmondsworth: Penguin.

Moorcock, Michael. 1983. Introduction to *New Worlds: An Anthology*, 9–26. London: Flamingo.

———. 2010. *Into the Media Web: Selected Short Non-Fiction, 1956–2006.* Ed. John Davey. Manchester: Savoy.

Nicholls, Peter. 1975. Jerry Cornelius at the Atrocity Exhibition: Anarchy and Entropy in *New Worlds* Science Fiction 1964–1974. *Foundation* 9: 22–44.

Nietzsche, Friedrich. 1998 (1873). On Truth and Lying in an Extra-Moral Sense. In *Literary Theory: An Anthology*, eds. Julie Rivkin and Michael Ryan, 358–361. Malden MA: Blackwell.

Poynor, Rick. 2014. The Conceptual Advertising of J.G. Ballard. *Design Observer*, April 17. https://designobserver.com/feature/the-conceptual-advertising-of-jg-ballard/38432 (accessed 20/02/24).

Sontag, Susan. 2001 (1966). *Against Interpretation*. London: Vintage.

Sweet, Matthew. 2023. *Free Thinking*, BBC Radio 3, December 7. https://www.bbc.co.uk/sounds/play/m001sw09 (accessed 25/02/24).

Tarshis, Jerome. 1973. Krafft-Ebing Visits Dealey Plaza: The Recent Fiction of J.G. Ballard. *Evergreen Review* 96. https://www.jgballard.ca/criticism/jgb_tarshis_ax1973.html (accessed 13/02/24).

Waugh, Patricia. 1984. *Metafiction: The Theory and Practice of Self-Conscious Fiction*. London: Methuen.

CHAPTER 4

Rogue Anthropology: *Crash*, Surrealism and the Independent Group

Abstract This chapter examines Ballard's relationship with Eduardo Paolozzi and the Independent Group, in particular, its use of anthropological techniques derived from Mass Observation as an arm of the British Surrealist movement. The chapter demonstrates not only how Ballard uses those devices to explore the post-war experience of suburbia but also how those methods are appropriated by the authoritarian persona of his antihero Vaughan.

Keywords Suburbia • Anthropology • Eduardo Paolozzi • Mass Observation • Surrealism

In 1972, possibly whilst Ballard was editing the manuscript of *Crash*, he was visited by the poet Pierre Joris and the translator Carl Weissner with regards to publishing a French translation of *The Atrocity Exhibition*. On their train back, the two Europeans 'looked out at the grey London burbs flitting by in their grime and apocalyptic desolation' and realised 'that Ballard was … a satiric realist: his worlds were starkly all around us' (Joris 2009). Yet although Ballard articulated his fear of the future in terms of a 'vast, conforming *suburb of the soul*' in which 'nothing new will happen' (*RS* 8), he also defended suburbia as 'the cutting-edge of social change': 'Everything started here – from the fitness crusade to wife-swapping' (quoted Vallely 1997). Although the idea of suburbia ultimately terrified him, in a characteristic move, Ballard was drawn to 'the social trends' encapsulating his adopted home of Shepperton: 'the whole video/word-processor thing – and it's very interesting to watch the fashions. I would almost call it an *airport culture* ... a very transient kind of world' (*RS* 14).

One critical response to this archetypal Ballardian landscape has been to draw on Marc Augé's (1995, 7) 'anthropology of the near'. Following David Harvey's postmodern account of space-time compression, Augé argues that neither private nor public memory are reliable markers but are engulfed by an 'overabundance of events' (28). Spatial distance dwindles and is supplanted by the proliferation of 'non-places': 'high-speed roads and railways, interchanges, airports ... the great commercial centres, or the extended transit camps where the planet's refugees are parked' (34). However, just as Ballard prefigures Jean Baudrillard's critique of *Crash*, so his narrator also anticipates Augé's thesis: 'I realised that the human inhabitants of this technological landscape no longer provided its sharpest pointers, its keys to the borderzones of identity ... all the hopes and fancies of this placid suburban enclave, drenched in a thousand infidelities, faltered before the solid reality of the motorway embankments' (*C* 48–9). Consequently, Andrzej Gasiorek's (2005, 87) observation that 'the conjunction of urban and bodily geometries opened up by technology ... is of principal interest, producing a stylised sexuality which takes its cue from curtain-walled office-blocks, ferrous motorway intersections, rectilinear apartment buildings, anonymous airport concourses, and abandoned car parks' merely redoubles what the text already says. To understand more effectively how *Crash* draws upon an anthropological critique, we need to contextualise the novel in terms of Ballard's émigré status and the extent to which anthropology had already been utilised by movements close to Ballard's interests in surrealism: the Independent Group (IG) and Mass Observation (MO).

Ballard's ambivalence towards English society was formed the moment he arrived at Southampton Docks in 1946, 'under a cold sky so grey and low', and peopled with inhabitants 'shabbily dressed and with a haunted air' (*ML* 121). As David Paddy (2015, 18) has noted, Ballard's disappointment with England mirrors those of Afro-Caribbean writers such as George Lamming and Samuel Selvon. Yet the poverty, self-delusion and stifling social mores that made England 'a very strange country' also provided 'fit subjects for analysis' in terms of its social and sexual repression (*FSS* 9). At the same time as Ballard entered The Leys School in Cambridge, he became fascinated by psychoanalysis and surrealism as potential keys for unlocking this social and psychological terrain. As he later admitted, 'I've treated England as if it were a strange fiction, and my task has been to elicit the truth' (*ML* 35); a process that began with the teenage Ballard attempting to learn the 'codes of behaviour' around which 'English middle-class life revolved' (125), and which continued in one of Ballard's first jobs after dropping out of university:

> Then I worked as an encyclopaedia salesman. That was fascinating, one of the most interesting periods in my life. … Simply going into people's homes, I was conducting my own Gallup survey of English life … it's quite extraordinary, the variety of human lives. (*FSS* 12)

In particular, Ballard noted how, with rising social mobility, the acquisition of consumer goods not only adorned but also redefined the domestic space: 'Information came through advertising and the television set. They would show off their huge new screens, their wall-to-wall carpeting and their modern kitchens and bathrooms … Consumerism provided all the bearings they needed in their lives' (*ML* 160). The commodity fetishism of the aspirant working classes seemed to confirm what Ballard had already noted in the appeal of American film noirs: 'a new kind of popular culture was emerging that played on the latent psychopathy of its audiences, and in fact needed to elicit that strain of psychopathy if it was to work' (148).

J.B. Priestley though, to whom the Ballardian phrase 'inner space' is often credited, had already detected in 1934 that there was not one but three Englands. First, a residual England of 'cathedrals and minsters and manor houses and inns' (Priestley 2018, 335), the bucolic myth that underwrote the colonial fantasy of the motherland. Second, a dominant England forged in the Industrial Revolution, consisting of a 'devastated countryside, sooty dismal little towns, and still sootier grim fortress-like cities' (336). But last, an emergent England whose 'real birth-place' is the US:

> This is the England of arterial and by-pass roads, of filling stations and factories that look like exhibition buildings, of giant cinemas and dance-halls and cafés, bungalows with tiny garages, cocktail bars, Woolworths… It is a large-scale, mass-production job, with cut prices … as near to a classless society as we have got yet. (338–9)

Despite his withering tone, Priestley sees this England as the coming society, 'a cleaner, tidier, healthier, saner world' (340), but 'lacking in character, in zest, gusto, flavour, bite, drive, originality': 'the perfect subjects for an iron autocracy' (341). As Ballard would later remark, 'in a totally sane society, madness is the only freedom' (*EM* 193).

Although Ballard was already a devotee of modern art, it was the exhibition *This is Tomorrow* at the Whitechapel Gallery in 1956 which galvanised his work. Ballard had already realised in 1954, whilst doing his National Service with the RAF in Canada, that genre SF, in the form of such magazines as *Galaxy* and *Fantasy & Science Fiction*, offered a better medium than modernist fiction for exploring 'the pathology that underlay the consumer society, the TV landscape and the nuclear arms race' (*ML* 167). In the 1950s, however, science fiction was often a pawn in the anti-Americanism that coloured debates around high and low culture. Arthur Koestler (1953, 891), writing about the formation of the British Science Fiction Club, commented that 'a new craze, a kind of cosmic jitterbug, has crossed the Atlantic' whilst similar disparaging comments were expressed on both the political Right (T.S. Eliot) and the political Left (Richard Hoggart). By contrast, the writers and artists associated with the IG, a collective that had met through the ICA between 1952 and 1955, were fascinated by US popular culture, and in particular science fiction: 'a higher order of imagination exists in a SF pulp produced on the outskirts of L.A. than the little magazines of today' (Paolozzi 1990, 185).

This is Tomorrow, in which the IG contributed to five of the twelve stands, confirmed for Ballard the correctness of his chosen path: 'for the first time the visitor to the Whitechapel saw the response of imaginations tuned to the visual culture of the street, to advertising, road signs, films and popular magazines, to the design of packaging and consumer goods' (*ML* 188). The IG had a strong interest in Dada and surrealism, both of which 'can be best understood through the broader context of mass media and its profound effect on perception and the question of reality' (Banash 2013, 133). The IG's use of collage, most famously Richard Hamilton's *Just What Is It That Makes Today's Homes So Different, So Appealing?* (1956), both incorporated and intervened in mass culture, revealing the intersections between sex, violence, consumerism and technology, as seen in Eduardo Paolozzi's series of screenprints, *BUNK!* (1947–1952). There were also explicit connections between members of the IG and pre-war modernism: in the late 1940s, Paolozzi lived in Paris and met several of the surrealists; Toni del Renzio had been part of the British surrealist movement in the late 1930s; and Nigel Henderson's mother, Wyn, had managed Nancy Cunard's Hours Press in Paris. Reyner Banham, who like Ballard later became a trustee of the New Arts Lab, elaborated on a machine ethos in essays such as 'Vehicles of Desire' (1955), where he eulogised over the styling of US automobiles in ways that prefigured Ballard's sexualisation of the motorcar (Dorrian 2018/2019). Both Lawrence Alloway and John McHale promoted the IG's practice in terms of an expanding cultural field that drew upon notions from cybernetics, semantics and anthropology.

It was no coincidence when Michael Moorcock approached Paolozzi to become *New Worlds*' 'Aeronautics Advisor' in 1967: a meaningless title but useful when negotiating the magazine's Arts Council grant. Although Paolozzi only contributed two illustrations to *New Worlds*, his presence informed its visual content, for example in the photomontages of Charles Platt, the Pop Art imagery of Pamela Zoline, and the juxtaposition of text and image in such stories as Ballard's 'The Summer Cannibals' (1969). There were immediate affinities between Paolozzi and the IG with *New Worlds*: a shared preoccupation in language systems; the merger between humans and machines; the spectacle of the consumer society; and the violent desire of an eroticised technology. Ballard, with whom Paolozzi formed a close bond, summarised their common interests in 1971:

> The subject matter of science fiction is the subject matter of everyday life: the gleam on refrigerator cabinets, the contours of a wife's or husband's thighs passing the newsreel images on a colour TV set, the conjunction of musculature and chromium artefact within an automobile interior, the unique postures of passengers on an airport escalator – all in all, close to the world of the Pop painters and sculptors, Paolozzi, Hamilton, Warhol, Wesselmann, Ruscha. (*UG* 207)

That same year, Ballard and Paolozzi were interviewed for the art magazine *Studio International*. Whilst Paolozzi acknowledged their shared aims, 'We're both involved with the encounter with machines, and we're both involved with forcing people to look' (*EM* 44), Ballard proposed a distinctly modernist conception of the artist. In contravention of the death of affect, induced by people's alienation from scientific understanding of the technologies that surround them, 'the role of the artist' is 'to connect the two': 'His subject matter is no longer the world of manner and the world of ordinary appearances. He has to illuminate the real world for the ordinary person, the new world which technology and communications have created' (45). Ballard elaborated further, likening Paolozzi to a 'scientist on safari, looking at the landscape, testing, putting sensors out, charting various parameters' (38), a role that Ballard also applied to that of the writer: 'All he can do is devise hypotheses and test them against the facts' (*C* 6).

Although the investigative gaze in Ballard's work has been compared with the quasi-scientific method of nineteenth-century naturalism (Stanley 2015) and the scopophilia of photography (Baxter 2008), critics tend to focus on the overlapping interests in technology, consumerism and sexuality between the IG and *New Worlds* (Brittain 2013). The much deeper affinity, though, is anthropology. Alloway (2006, 173) argued that artists should regard 'our own, our present, society in a way analogous to anthropology', with particular attention paid to the social usages, cultural vocabularies and mass consumption. This approach would expand 'the limits of taste' (173) beyond the formalism that dominated modernist art criticism, just as Ballard felt the mainstream novel was constrained by psychological realism. Alloway's proposal, though, was prefigured by MO's injunction in 1937: 'How little we know of our next-door neighbour and his habits; how little we know of ourselves. Of conditions of life and thought in another class or another district, our ignorance is complete. The anthropology of ourselves is still only a dream' (quoted Spencer 2012, 319). MO's desire to 'decipher the overlooked signs and symbols structuring the shared everyday environment' (319) was replicated in Ballard's own need 'to explain the significance of mysterious and apparently unrelated objects, this huge network of ciphers and encoded instructions … that surround us in reality' (*RS* 43).

The reading of symbols, though, was already present in the prehistory of surrealism: 'we who understand the signs of the metaphysical alphabet, know what joys and sorrows are hidden within a portico, the angle of a street or even a room, on the surface of a table, between the sides of a box' (Chirico 1968, 452). Formed in 1936, MO arose from the main intellectual currents that characterised pre-war surrealism whilst remaining distinct from the 'ethnographic surrealism' ascribed to figures such as Georges Bataille, Michel Leiris and Marcel Mauss (Clifford 1981). For Ballard, the importance of surrealism lay not in its irrational content but in its approach to that material: 'the analytic function of the sciences as a means of codifying the inner experience of the senses' that reveals 'the inner reality of our lives' (*UG* 85). Although Ballard was aware of the British surrealists of the

1930s (*RS* 23), his principal interests lay in Europe and visual rather than literary surrealism. However, Henderson and his anthropologist wife Judith had conducted written and photographic surveys of everyday life in Bethnal Green on behalf of the sociologist, J.L. Petersen, which blended with the IG's interest in 'multiple sign systems' (Spencer 2012, 323). Ballard too conducted an idiosyncratic kind of fieldwork for *Crash* by taking numerous photographs of motorway architecture (Holliday 2017).

MO announced itself in a letter to *The New Statesman* on 30 January 1937, signed by its three principal figures: the surrealist poet Charles Madge, the anthropologist Tom Harrisson and the documentary filmmaker Humphrey Jennings. They sought to recruit five-thousand observers to record the thoughts and feelings, habits and customs of working-class people, so as to make manifest the latent desires of the socially disenfranchised. As Nick Hubble (2006, 60–1) has noted, Madge was deeply influenced by the unorthodox anthropologist Gregory Bateson, who argued that the consistent mapping of affective responses could reveal the underlying *eidos* ('essence' or 'species') of the wider culture.[1] This revolutionary appeal contrasted with the more technically minded Harrisson; the tension of which can be found in their strangely worded list of 'problems':

> Behaviour of people at war memorials
> Shouts and gestures of motorists
> The aspidistra cult
> Anthropology of football pools
> Bathroom behaviour
> Beards, armpits, eyebrows
> Anti-semitism
> Distribution, diffusion and significance of the dirty joke
> Funerals and undertakers
> Female taboos about eating
> The private lives of midwives (quoted Jackson 2004, 184)

The random juxtaposition of items, in which one image is superimposed upon another, resembles a surrealist poem. In particular, it recalls the innovative use of the litany by one of the original MO observers, David Gascoyne (1994, 23), in his poem 'And the Seventh Dream is the Dream of Isis' (1933):

> teach children to sin at the age of five
> to cut out the eyes of their sisters with nail-scissors
> to run into the streets and offer themselves to unfrocked priests
> teach insects to invade the deathbeds of rich spinsters

Or, indeed, the almost baffling construction of Ballard's prose: 'I think of the crashes of excited schizophrenics colliding head-on into stalled laundry vans in one-way streets; of manic-depressives crushed while making pointless U-turns on motorway access roads; of luckless paranoids driving at full speed into the brick walls at the ends of known cul-de-sacs' (*C* 15).

The use of the litany form, a device not found within French surrealist poetry, has several effects. First, it is paratactical—the syntactical structure characteristic of both modernist literature and holy scripture—so that ideas or images are juxtaposed with one another without a causal link. Second, being a list of declarations, the litany evokes an orderly succession even though the individual items may have no obvious connection. Third, the litany is incantatory—literally so in a church service where it is designed to be recited by the priest and congregation—so that, although the reader is experiencing James's interior monologue, the form of the writing is immersive and draws us in as a participant. Fourth, despite this seductive effect, the litany is aphoristic, derived from the Greek *apo* (meaning 'away') and *horos* (meaning 'a boundary'), so that the individual items collide with the self-imposed limit of the incantation and seek to separate. Fifth, due to this instability, the litany is at once excessively meaningful (sacred and divine) and profoundly meaningless (boring and tedious). Last, and as such, the litany provides what Walter Benjamin termed the 'profane illumination' of surrealist writing, 'a materialistic, anthropological inspiration' (1979, 227), which invokes the mysterious within the quotidian, a breakout that Benjamin, like Ballard, sees in terms of the marriage between body, technology and symbol: 'all revolutionary tension becomes collective bodily innervation, and all the bodily innervations of the collective become revolutionary discharge' (239). For Madge, MO's compiling of subaltern voices and latent desires constituted a political challenge to bourgeois orthodoxy. For the IG, the intermeshing of bodies, artefacts and commodities enabled the recuperation of human value within a vast information network. For Ballard's characters, the discovery of 'a new sexuality born from a perverse technology' (*C* 13) seems to transcend the 'coming autogeddon' (*C* 106); what Alloway (2006, 74) refers to as mass culture's 'assault on the body' via its graphic imagery and sensory overload.

And yet, despite the imagery of flight in the novel, most notably during James's acid trip when he sees cars 'soaring along the causeways on wings of fire' (*C* 209), the characters fail to escape their situation. Although James lends a tragic sublimity to Vaughan's death, describing both its 'logic and beauty' (*C* 222), Vaughan fails to strike either his intended target or to take flight successfully: he 'had been travelling along the open deck of the flyover at the car's maximum speed, trying to launch himself into the sky' (*C* 222). Moreover, Vaughan has earlier been frustrated by the car-crash of his henchman Seagrave, dressed as an imitation of Elizabeth Taylor, which 'pre-empted that real death which Vaughan had preserved for himself' (*C* 187). By contrast, in a move akin to the surrealistic work of Angela Carter,[2] Ballard's fiction is at its most transgressive when he foregrounds the limits of his characters' transgression. Instead of breaking through to a nebulous outside, their failure to do so reveals their inherited constraints, wherein lies Ballard's anthropological critique.

As Paddy (2015, 88) has argued, Ballard's 1960s fiction was engaged with 'the twin phenomena of consumer capitalism and the electronic media … operating together as a new form of psychological imperialism'. However, whereas *The Atrocity Exhibition* explored the fusion of the respective dreamworlds of its protagonist and commodity culture, *Crash* utilises the latter as the ambient noise against which its characters play out their loveless lives: 'television newsreels of wars and student riots, natural disasters and police brutality which we vaguely watched on the colour TV set in our bedroom as we masturbated each other' (*C* 37). The arid sex-life of James and Catherine at the start of the novel is in inverse proportion to which the spectacle occupies everyday life. At the same time, though, the narrative is also interested in how that surface reality is materially produced. Whereas in *The Atrocity Exhibition* Elizabeth Taylor is a godlike figure mimetised on huge billboards, in *Crash*, although deified by James, she is an actual person filming a TV advert:

> Already she was assuming the postures of a crash victim, her fingers weakly touching the streaks of carmine resin on her knees, thighs delicately raised from the plastic seat cover as if flinching from some raw mucous membrane. (*C* 108)

In a perverse premonition of the death scene that Vaughan imagines for her, the 'high-budget film' publicising Ford's 'sports car range' (*C* 35) has merged into Taylor sitting in a crushed Citroën, suggesting that the titular car crash can itself be co-opted for the all-consuming spectacle. Yet while James fixates on the movie actress, the attention is drawn to other players in the mise-en-scène: the make-up artist; the sound engineer; the assistant producer; James's secretary and lover Renata; and (unseen but by implication present) the camera crew and the director Aida James. Whereas in *The Atrocity Exhibition* the spectacle appears to be floatless and free-forming, in *Crash* there is an almost Brechtian insistence upon the spectacle's material production, just as the novel is tethered to a discernible location in Greater London. Taylor herself, although unvoiced, is more than just a simulacrum: 'the crushed vehicle' seems 'to transform' around 'the unique contours of her body and personality' (*C* 109), a mysterious radiance that emanates from somewhere other than the manufactured spectacle.

Arguably, it is this glamour—literally, a spell or enchantment—that Vaughan seeks to both break and possess through Taylor's physical destruction: 'her uterus pierced by the heraldic beak of the manufacturer's medallion, his semen emptying across the luminescent dials' (*C* 8). Although James ascribes a 'personal glamour' to Vaughan, it arises from his physical armature: 'heavy black hair over a scarred face, an American combat jacket … an aggressive lecture-theatre manner and complete conviction in his subject-matter' (*C* 63). Instead, Vaughan exhibits charisma: a dynamism that binds his acolytes to him. Whereas Taylor is defined by her stillness, such that she melts into the role of a car crash victim and bends the environment around her, Vaughan is always active, disguising himself as hospital staff, pushing his way into crash scenes, continually taking photographs that he arranges 'with the devotion of an Earl Marshal' (*C* 7), imposing his sexuality upon others, and driving like 'an ugly machine sprung from a trap' (*C* 8). In his role as 'hoodlum scientist' (*C* 19), Vaughan's claims to leadership do not stem from legal or traditional forms of authority, in the Weberian sense of those terms, but purely from force of will. As James remarks, 'Vaughan annexes people to him. There's still a strong element of the TV personality about his whole style' (*C* 116). James connects Vaughan's past as a minor media celebrity with his extension of the colonising tendencies of the spectacle. For Vaughan is both a coloniser and a seer. On the one hand, he implants 'the idea' of the celebrity car crash in Seagrave's 'head' (*C* 115); on the other hand, Vaughan reveals to James the truth of his sexual desires through the photographic narrative he has assembled. The paradox of Vaughan's purposes not only confuses those around him but also plays upon their confusion, binding them to his will. James 'uneasily' prepares magnifications of Taylor's body parts on his office photocopier, handing them to Vaughan like 'a death warrant' (*C* 8), but he does so nonetheless.

Taylor and Vaughan therefore embody two aspects of seductive personality. One which, despite its opaqueness, can be instrumentalised as part of the spectacle's Apollonian stylisation of all things; the other which, in its grotesquerie, represents the Dionysiac surplus of commodity culture: the 'nightmare angel of the expressways' (*C* 84). Whereas Taylor's body can be decorated with fake wounds that appear to be seamless, Vaughan's visage is a horrific collage: 'His features looked as if they had been displaced laterally, reassembled after the crash from a collection of faded publicity photographs' (*C* 64). The all-too-visible suturing of Vaughan's wounds foregrounds the violence that Taylor's make-up alludes to but homogenises. It is ironic then, when Seagrave kills himself, the initial police broadcasts make 'garbled references to the multiple injuries of the screen actress, Elizabeth Taylor' (*C* 184). Vaughan's physical deformity, however, does not signify him as society's avenging Id. Rather, the authoritarianism that was already there, cultivated through his early TV exposure, is amplified by the wounds that Vaughan uses to intrigue those around him.

Vaughan effectively colonises the minds of his entourage by playing upon their previous experiences of car crashes; through persuasion and seduction; his calculated performance as a 'frustrated actor' (*C* 88); the totemic presence of his wounds like 'a cuneiform of the flesh' (*C* 90) and his phallic authority; copious amounts of hashish; and his quixotic mood swings: 'by turns aggressive, distracted, sensitive, clumsy, absorbed and brutal' (*C* 89). In this regard, Vaughan not only complements the colonisation of everyday life by the spectacle but also echoes the imperial myth of the self-reliant coloniser who bends the indigenous population to his will: early on in his narration, James imagines Helen and her husband 'ransacking' each 'other's body like Crusoe stripping his ship' (*C* 44). Since the reader only ever sees Vaughan from James's perspective, the disappointed suburbanite maps onto Vaughan his ideal conception of masculinity derived from the kinds of imperial literature that Ballard himself read in his youth: Daniel Defoe, G.A. Henty, Charles Kingsley, Robert Louis Stevenson (*FFS* 5–6). This mapping is partially due to James's 'responses' being 'pre-empted' by Vaughan's self-performance (*C* 88), a mask that like his damaged features renders Vaughan indecipherable. In James's gratitude for the compensation that Vaughan brings to his affluent yet barren existence, there remains a residual desire for the dullness of suburbia to be rekindled. For Ballard, this spark was to be found in the architecture of the Westway, 'a virtual city-state borne on a rush of radial tyres' (*SN* 311), but for James, it is mediated through the lingering dreamwork of an imperial fantasy, a 'postcolonial melancholia' that has been found elsewhere in British SF of the 1970s (Luckhurst 2005, 172–80).

Lastly, although Ballard sees in the surreal uses of anthropology a key to unlock the prison of English social life, he is also aware that it too can be co-opted by the authoritarian personality. At one point Vaughan compiles a series of questionnaires based upon the responses of his entourage and those who come within his orbit: computer programmers, medical staff, airport stewardesses. As sociologists such as C. Wright Mills and Max Weber have observed, the questionnaire can act as an instrument of bureaucracy and social control (Dillon 2023, 21–2). Yet it also played a vital role, alongside other data-harvesting techniques, in the history of MO and the adoption of anthropological procedures by the IG. Consequently, Vaughan's use of the questionnaire not only assembles data from his subjects, it also appropriates surreal methodologies in order to extend his control over their latent desires. Most prominently, the questionnaire uses the list or litany form. The respondent is given a selection of celebrities, randomly chosen, 'and invited to devise an imaginary car-crash in which one of them might die' (*C* 132). The ensuing 'choice of wounds and death-modes' is one long litany, possibly culled from Jacob Kulowski's textbook, but which, in its obsessiveness, becomes increasingly surreal: 'injuries caused by specialist automobile accessories such as record players, cocktail cabinets and radio-telephones' (*C* 133). This obsession spills over into the next list, 'genital wounds caused during automobile accidents', which 'photocopied', 'extracted' or 'torn' from 'journals', 'reports', and memoranda, and juxtaposing text with image, resembles a collage (*C* 133–4). Both their content and jagged compilation signify 'units in a new currency of pain and desire' (*C* 134). James only focuses on the responses of Vaughan's immediate circle, especially those of Seagrave that describe 'an abattoir of sexual mutilation' (*C* 135). What is already an unrepresentative sample is therefore cherry-picked by James; as an anthropological inquiry, its results are worthless. But as an insight into an authoritarian mindset, and how that cognitive dissonance can be communicated to a group through the confusion of scientific and pseudo-scientific registers, Vaughan's questionnaire is illuminating. Focusing on how the celebrity bodies are both marked and itemised, becoming a series of modular units, James concludes that 'Vaughan or his volunteer subjects would have mounted [Taylor's] body in any number of bizarre postures … the cars in which she moved would become devices for exploiting every pornographic and erotic possibility, every conceivable sex-death and mutilation' (*C* 136–7). It is to the nature of this autopsy that we now turn.

Notes

1. Following his departure to the US, Bateson became a key figure in the development of cybernetics which in turn influenced the IG alongside the semantic theories of Alfred Korzybski (Massey 1995, 85–6). Both O'Hara (2012) and Poli (2016) have argued for the similarities between Ballard and Bateson's thought.
2. In her speech at Eastercon in 1982, Carter (1997, 34) commented that 'I could relate instantly to the world of Ballard's *Crash*. … That was how it felt to be living through the margin of the Vietnam War.'

Works Cited

Alloway, Lawrence. 2006. *Imagining the Present: Context, Content, and the Role of the Critic*, ed. Richard Kalina. London: Routledge.
Augé, Marc. 1995. *Non-Places: Introduction to an Anthropology of Supermodernity*. Trans. John Howe. London: Verso.
Banash, David. 2013. *Collage Culture*. Amsterdam: Rodopi.
Baxter, Jeannette. 2008. Radical Surrealism: Rereading Photography and History in J.G. Ballard's *Crash*. *Textual Practice* 22 (3): 507–528.
Benjamin, Walter. 1979 (1929). Surrealism: The Last Snapshot of the European Intelligentsia. In *One-Way Street and Other Writings*, trans. Edmund Jephcott and Kingsley Shorter, 225–239. London: New Left Books.
Brittain, David. 2013. *Eduardo Paolozzi at New Worlds: Science Fiction and Art in the Sixties*. Manchester: Savoy Books.
Carter, Angela. 1997. *Shaking a Leg: Collected Journalism and Writings*. Ed. Jenny Uglow. London: Chatto and Windus.
Chirico, Giorgio de. 1968 (1919). On Metaphysical Art. In *Theories of Modern Art*, ed. Herschel B. Chipp, 448–453. Berkeley: University of California Press.
Clifford, James. 1981. On Ethnographic Surrealism. *Comparative Studies in Society and History* 23 (4): 539–564.
Dillon, Tom. 2023. A Brief History of *New Worlds* in Four Forms. *Foundation* 144: 20–35.
Dorrian, Mark. 2018/2019. Banham avec Ballard: On Style and Violence. *Cabinet* 66. https://www.cabinetmagazine.org/issues/66/dorrian.php (accessed 24/04/24).
Gascoyne, David. 1994. *Selected Poems*. London: Enitharmon Press.
Gasiorek, Andrzej. 2005. *J.G. Ballard*. Manchester: Manchester University Press.
Holliday, Mike. 2017. Taking the Top Off His Skull: The Genesis of J.G. Ballard's *Crash*. https://www.holli.co.uk/crash.htm (accessed 15/02/24).
Hubble, Nick. 2006. *Mass Observation and Everyday Life: Culture, History, Theory*. Basingstoke: Palgrave Macmillan.

Jackson, Kevin. 2004. *Humphrey Jennings*. London: Picador.
Joris, Pierre. 2009. J.G. Ballard (1930–2009). *Nomadics*, April 20. https://pierrejoris.com/blog/jg-ballard-1930-2009/ (accessed 12/04/24).
Koestler, Arthur. 1953. The Literature of Boredom. *The Listener* 48: 891.
Luckhurst, Roger. 2005. *Science Fiction*. Cambridge: Polity Press.
Massey, Anne. 1995. *The Independent Group: Modernism and Mass Culture in Britain, 1945–*. Manchester: Manchester University Press.
O'Hara, Dan. 2012. Reading Posture and Gesture in Ballard's Novels. In *J.G. Ballard: Visions and Revisions*, ed. Jeannette Baxter and Rowland Wymer, 105–120. Basingstoke: Palgrave Macmillan.
Paddy, David Ian. 2015. *The Empires of J.G. Ballard: An Imagined Geography*. Canterbury: Gylphi.
Paolozzi, Eduardo. 1990. Notes from a Lecture at the Institute of Contemporary Arts, 1958. In *The Independent Group: Postwar Britain and the Aesthetics of Plenty*, ed. David Robbins, 183–185. Cambridge MA: MIT Press.
Poli, Guglielmo. 2016. Geometries of the Imagination: The Map-Territory Relation in *The Atrocity Exhibition*. In *J.G. Ballard: Landscapes of Tomorrow*, ed. Richard Brown et al., 87–98. Amsterdam: Rodopi.
Priestley, J.B. 2018 (1934). *English Journey*. Bradford: Great Northern Books.
Spencer, Catherine. 2012. The Independent Group's "Anthropology of Ourselves". *Art History* 35 (2): 314–335.
Stanley, Rachel. 2015. "The scientist on safari": J.G. Ballard and the Naturalist Gaze. *Textual Practice* 29 (6): 1165–1185.
Vallely, Paul. 1997. Living: It's New, It's Modern, It's Subtopia. *The Independent*, October 10. https://www.independent.co.uk/life-style/living-it-s-new-it-s-modern-it-s-subtopia-1235314.html (accessed 19/04/24).

CHAPTER 5

Body Horrors: Cyborgs, Reptiles and Mongrels

Abstract This chapter argues that, while postmodern responses to *Crash* have stressed the cyborg as mechanical hybrid, the novel also emphasises the links between human and non-human animals. In exploring this connection, the chapter compares *Crash* with the evolutionary theories to be found in Ballard's earlier novel, *The Drowned World*. *Crash* contrasts three different conceptions of human behaviour, each rooted in evolutionary theory, to be found in the work of Carl Jung, Arthur Koestler and B.F. Skinner. These models each reflect critically upon the desire for transcendence embodied by Vaughan. What he seeks to transcend is the corporeal, associated not only with the animalistic, but also with those regarded as bare life: prostitutes and migrants.

Keywords Non-human animals • Evolution • Psychoanalysis • Neurology • Behaviourism

Reflecting on the period that produced *Crash*, Ballard commented: 'people were becoming dehumanised and overcerebralised; emotional responses to everything were becoming so stylised that we were moving into a kind of mad Nazi world' (*IT* 22). To make sense of this creeping fascism, Ballard often compared himself to that of an anatomist: 'I'm assembling the materials of an autopsy, and I'm treating reality ... almost as if it were a cadaver, or ... the contents of a special kind of forensic inquisition. *We have these objects here – what are they?*' (*RS* 42). Whilst this metaphor drew upon Ballard's training as a medical student, it also reiterated associations between the realist author and the anatomist, from Gustave Flaubert to Emile Zola via Ivan Turgenev (1998, 80): 'What a sumptuous body she's got!' Basarov continued. 'I'd just love to get her into an anatomical theatre'. The objectification of the body persisted from the early twentieth-century avant-garde, 'to see everything, even man, in its quality of *thing*' (Chirico 1968, 397), to the *nouveau roman* that inspired Ballard's contemporaries, most notably Brian Aldiss: 'interiority is put in parentheses; objects, spaces, and man's circulation among them are promoted to the rank of subjects' (Barthes 1972, 23). To regard the human body as no more than a moveable part within an increasingly technologised terrain, 'the landscape of my life was now bounded by a continuous artificial horizon' (*C* 53), repositions it as a node in some vast cybernetic system: 'The wounds on my knees and chest were beacons tuned to a series of beckoning transmitters, carrying the signals ... which would unlock this immense stasis and free these drivers for the real destinations set for their vehicles, the paradises of the electric highway' (*C* 53).

In one of the few pieces to consider the role of Darwinian theory in *Crash*, Erica Moore (2014, 41) suggests that the novel not only evokes 'human-machine integration and intercourse' but also the 'evolutionary potential for the future of the human'. As Moore indicates, the merger between man and machine has rendered *Crash* prime material for the transhumanist movement as it has developed from the early 1960s. James's sex acts with the mechanically assisted Gabrielle in her specially designed car are exemplary in this regard:

> I moved my hands from her pubis to the scars on her thighs, feeling the tender causeways driven through her flesh by the handbrake of the car in which she had crashed. My right arm held her shoulders, feeling the impress of the contoured leather, the meeting points of hemispherical and rectilinear geometries. I explored the scars on her thighs and arms, feeling for the wound areas under her left breast, as she in turn explored mine, deciphering together these codes of a sexuality made possible by our two car-crashes. (*C* 178–9)

However, whereas the 'exploratory ordeal' (*C* 176) of their sex acts is forensic in its detail, forming 'templates for new genital organs, the moulds of sexual possibilities yet to be created' (*C* 177), the postmodern and transhumanist readings that once dominated criticism of *Crash* instrumentalise such speculations according to their own agendas. This instrumentality has the potential to become the armoured techno-fascist body that Hal Foster (1991), drawing upon Klaus Theweleit's investigation of German World War I soldier diaries, sees as in dialogue with the work of Hans Bellmer and Max Ernst, artists both important to Ballard. More recently, Rachel Murray (2020, 14) has argued that modernism's attraction to exoskeletal structures, although 'bound up with axioms of resistant hardness, exteriority and self-protection', also sought 'to develop forms of expression ... robust enough to survive the descent into industrial warfare and rapid modernization but also adaptable to the relentless pace of social and technological change'. Much the same could also be said for the protagonists of *Crash* and their relationship to the technological sensorium. Subsequent approaches, which focus on Ballard's abject or grotesque treatment of the body (Whiting 2012; Sage 2008), emphasise that they both disrupt the reader's position and the novel's closed, formal construction (Kavanagh 2019). Instead of Paul Youngquist's claim (2000) that in *Crash* 'the body becomes conceptualised', the visceral content foregrounds its 'fragility' and 'spillability of ... essential juices' (Carter 1993, 47): blood, semen, vomit and mucus.

To that end, then, we need to focus less on the man-machine hybrid that forms one aspect of Donna Haraway's 'cyborg manifesto' and more on the other: the 'breached' borderline 'between human and animal' where instead of 'walling of ... people from other living beings, cyborgs signal disturbingly and pleasurably tight coupling' (Haraway 1985, 66). We have already noted how Ballard fictionalised those close to him; as a dog-owner, he did the same. Although references are made to the dead and the dying at the start of *Crash*, the first actual death the reader sees is that of a dog: 'The impact of its body, like a padded hammer, and the shower of glass as the animal was carried over the roof, convinced me that we were about to die' (*C* 12). Vaughan's refusal to stop, and his anger at 'brushing the beads of frosted glass from his cheeks' (*C* 12), is in contrast with the dispassion that he photographs dying humans or manipulates the limbs of prostitutes in rehearsal of 'the deformed anatomies of vehicle crash victims' (*C* 145). The dog represents an unplanned death; a chance occurrence that Vaughan seeks to nullify through his own 'random' violent acts (*C* 12).

Vaughan kills a second dog off-stage; the 'gummy residue' and 'heavy dent' (*C* 157) are spotted by James, who recalls a similar incident when he struck 'a German shepherd dog' that ran 'blindly across a street' (*C* 157–8). On that occasion, James halted and 'walked back to find two schoolgirls vomiting into their hands over the dying dog' (*C* 158). Their visceral reaction contrasts now with James's response who only regards the bloodstains as potential police evidence. James is not only complicit in Vaughan's actions but also his worldview where some deaths count more than others:

> The long triangular grooves on the car had been formed within the death of an unknown creature, its vanished identity abstracted in terms of the geometry of this vehicle. How much more mysterious would be our own deaths, and those of the famous and powerful? (*C* 13)

But the dog is neither 'vanished' nor 'abstracted', yet recurs and merges with Vaughan's identity. As Vaughan's desire to turn Elizabeth Taylor into the subject of his conceptual death becomes more desperate, so James desires to 'take his body in my hands, like that of some vagrant dog, and anneal its wounds' (*C* 148). Following Seagrave's death, Vaughan mentally and physically deteriorates, picking at his scabs and moving 'in bursts of exhausted nervousness … like an uncomfortable animal' (*C* 192). Yet, although Vaughan has 'the look of an unsuccessful fanatic', he 'doggedly' holds 'together his spent obsessions' (*C* 193).

Although Ballard once remarked that 'to establish one's own freedom', the individual had to perform 'some perverse act', even if it's just … *kicking the dog*' (*RS* 15), Vaughan's canine transformation suggests the opposite: the evaporation of his imagined death 'in a simultaneous automobile disaster, millions of vehicles hurled together in a terminal congress of spurting loins and engine coolant' (*C* 16) within the confines of his own animalistic body. Roger Luckhurst (1997, 126), in critiquing the postmodern responses to Ballard's fiction, has argued that from this perspective 'the *immanence* of all signs, their endless re-duplication, becomes the defining signature of Ballard, displacing the narratives of *transcendence* that had previously governed his work.' By contrast, not only is there continuity between Ballard's natural and urban catastrophes but the tension between transcendence and immanence, as dramatised in the relationship between the human and non-human animal, is also inscribed into *Crash*.

This tension is most notably seen in the recurring metaphor of the matador. This figure not only nods to another of Ballard's influences, Ernest Hemingway, but also embodies one of his favourite aphorisms: to immerse oneself in 'the destructive element ... and with the exertion of your hands and feet ... make the deep, deep sea keep you up' (Conrad 2002, 134). In adapting to and mastering the non-human, the matador is a transcendent figure, such as the pedestrians who, in the after-effects of James's acid trip, inhabit the crystalline landscape in 'suits of lights, as if I were a solitary visitor in a city of matadors' (*C* 209). Yet, in failing to adapt, the matador's fate is one of immanence; of being brought into contact with their corporeality. James describes himself as 'a gored bullfighter' (*C* 23) after he is cut free from his car crash. Seagrave, following his failed attempt to recreate 'a Spectacular Road Accident' (*C* 85), is likened to 'a myopic bullfighter running straight on to the bull's horns' (*C* 86). In death, his body is a mirror-image to those transcendent figures, 'dressed in its coronation armour of fractured glass, a suit of lights like a dead matador's' (*C* 186); 'already crystallizing, at last escaping out of this uneasy set of dimensions into a more beautiful universe' (*C* 185). Beside him, in ironic juxtaposition, lies the 'black wig', 'like a dead cat' (*C* 185). As Gregory Stephenson (1991, 71–3) notes, the novel's luminous and crystalline imagery echoes the eternal stasis of *The Crystal World* (1966) whilst also girding the theme of transfiguration as conveyed through the imagery of flight, sacrifice and ritual. However, the transcendence that Stephenson recounts is always held in suspension with its dialectical counterpart—immanence—or, better still, actively operates through it: an immanent transcendence.

For the Marxist and psychoanalyst Erich Fromm (1963, 36), the human need 'to transcend the role of the creature' takes one of two routes: creativity or destruction. Ballard, though, complicates this either-or by figuring a transcendence through the non-human organism. During the course of James's revelatory acid trip, 'the marker lines diving and turning' form 'a maze of white snakes, writhing as they carried the wheels of the cars crossing their backs, as delighted as dolphins' (*C* 196). Despite the elision between the 'angular contours' and 'unexpected junctions' of Gabrielle's body with 'the strange geometry' of her car (*C* 176), James describes their union as 'the fauna of a metal dream' (*C* 178). Vaughan regards clitorises as 'botanical specimens' (*C* 182); James refers to Renata's vulva as 'a wet flower' (*C* 56); 'the world ... flower[s] into wounds' (*C* 146). Despite James's clinical narration, with only Catherine and Seagrave making colloquial references to the sex act and the female anatomy, the sexual descriptions are characterised by the physicality of the verbs, such as 'pressing', 'pumping', 'driving', 'jerking', 'gasping', which suggest the animalistic qualities that James's narration omits. Whereas James imagines the human-machine-animal hybrid in pastoral terms, 'the coloured carapaces of the thousands of cars moved like the welcoming centaurs of some Arcadian land' (*C* 166), its carnality is fantasised as the flies which, in James's drug-induced hallucination, cover 'Vaughan's face, hovering around his mouth and nostrils as if waiting for the rancid liquors distilled from the body of a corpse' (*C* 204). The insect, then, captures the paradox of bodily transcendence: on the one hand, its exoskeleton evokes the impervious automobile carapace or James's attraction to Vaughan's 'hard' yet disfigured body (*C* 173); on the other hand, flies suggest the inchoate multiplicity that Vaughan seeks to transcend in the first place—the unplanned chaos embodied by his first victim, the mongrel dog. Paradoxically, then, the ground from which Vaughan tries to transcend is itself revealed to be groundless: the only way through is via the immanence that Vaughan's transcendent desire repudiates.

Instead, Vaughan's ultimate failure reveals his motivations to be reptilian; he is even compared to a reptile (*C* 103). In Ballard's first major novel *The Drowned World* (1962), the scientist Bodkin considers the neurological effects of the transformed environment:

> Is it only the external landscape which is altering? How often recently most of us have had the feeling of déjà vu, of having seen all this before, in fact of remembering these swamps and lagoons all too well. ... Every step we've taken in our evolution is a milestone inscribed with organic memories... Each one of us is as old as the entire biological kingdom, and our bloodstreams are tributaries of the great sea of its total memory. The uterine odyssey of the growing foetus recapitulates the entire evolutionary past, and its central nervous system is a coded time scale, each nexus of neurones and each spinal level marking a symbolic station, a unit of neuronic time. (*DW* 43–4)

Not only does this passage invoke the evolutionary theories of Ernst Haeckel, it also concedes that evolution can just as equally regress as progress. For Bodkin, this is a threatening prospect: 'If we let these buried phantoms master us as they re-appear we'll be swept back helplessly in the flood-tide like pieces of flotsam' (*DW* 44–5). Bodkin's colleague, the protagonist Kerans, does precisely that: responding to the 'mesmeric pull of the baying reptiles' (*DW* 71), in what turns out to be 'an ancient organic memory millions of years old' (*DW* 74), he adapts to the primordial environment and heads in the direction of 'the increasing rain and heat' (*DW* 175).

Ballard insisted that, for Kerans and James, the conclusions to *The Drowned World* and *Crash* were 'psychologically fulfilling' (*DM* 91) in a Jungian sense, since both characters finally integrate their conscious and unconscious lives with the collective unconscious mediated by the archetypal symbols of the sun or the automobile. Carl Jung speculated, however, that the combined effects of the Reformation, the Enlightenment and the Industrial Revolution had disintegrated the individual psyche, producing a 'mass man', 'isolated socially from other men, separated from his unconscious and his instincts, and therefore vulnerable to psychic epidemics, of which mass political movements are the most characteristic and virulent manifestation' (Odajnyk 1976, 40). Despite the romantic hypothesis of a prelapsarian moment, Jung's critique of psychic disintegration complements the influence of Wyndham Lewis on Ballard's work, whilst the implication that repressed or surplus libidinal energies will coalesce around a charismatic leader is clearly seen in James's devotion to Vaughan. Most importantly, Jung's understanding of brain development was also indebted to the evolutionary theories of Haeckel:

> This brain is inherited from its ancestors; it is the deposit of the psychic functioning of the whole human race. The child therefore brings with it an organ ready to function in the same way as it has functioned throughout human history. In the brain the instincts are performed, and so are the primordial images which have always been the basis of man's thinking. (19)

For Ballard, speaking in 2000 in the wake of such neo-Darwinists as Helena Cronin and Richard Dawkins, the motorised landscape is a manifestation of unacknowledged primal energies:

> I watch a theatre of the road taking place as young men in their hotted-up cars overtake young women in their hotted-up cars. You can see that the technology is facilitating all kinds of suppressed aggressions. (*EM* 377)

This amplification is aided in *Crash* by the surrounding environment. As Ballard acknowledged in 1974, the network of intersections, junctions and ring-roads is set into a 'marine landscape … infested with reservoirs and settling beds and conduits and little private canals' (*IT* 16), a water world whose psychological terrain seeps into the technological landscape. At the same time, the surplus libidinal desires that technology facilitates are fed back to the already disintegrated psyche, so that what the individual experiences is a conflation between manifest and latent desires, where there is no clear distinction between what constitutes external reality and private fantasy. This blurred borderline is what Jung calls 'psychic inflation' where an individual comes to identify with the collective unconscious and over-extends their ego, assuming a superhuman or godlike persona (Odajnyk 1976, 18). In the final stages of his mental deterioration, Vaughan retreats 'into his own skull' (*C* 16), an over-lit and violent realm where, as James imagines, 'Vaughan's semen bathed the entire landscape, powering these thousands of engines, electric circuits and private destinies, irrigating the smallest gestures of our lives' (*C* 191).

Arthur Koestler, too, was preoccupied with where these psychological dysfunctions would ultimately lead. In *The Ghost in the Machine* (1967), Koestler popularised Paul MacLean's triune model of brain development, now largely discredited, but still cited as part of pop psychology (Vale 2005, 23). In this model, the brain is divided into three: the 'neo-mammalian' and 'palaeomammalian', in which the higher functions such as language, memory, emotion and abstract reason are located, and the phylogenetically older 'reptilian' brain that governs more basic functions such as hunger, thirst and sexual desire. Koestler's argument (1967, 273–4) was that psychological dysfunction stemmed from the poor communication between these three regions of the brain, each evolving at different times and superimposed upon one another. Building upon this neurological dichotomy, Koestler argued that humans were motivated by two mutual needs: one for self-assertion, the other for self-transcendence. Working in harmony with each other, these needs enabled the individual to be both an autonomous being and an active social member of their family, nation or community (228–30). But, because of the miscommunication between the younger and older parts of the brain, humans were prone to paranoia or delusion, such that their needs became unbalanced and pathological. Crucially, the desire for self-transcendence was arguably 'more dangerous than' humanity's 'self-assertive tendencies' (233) since humans were willing to suspend their individual moralities and subordinate themselves to the collective will in pursuit of an ideal, myth or symbol at the expense of all others. As Jung suggests, the rise of instrumental reason only accelerated this process; as Koestler writes:

> Religious wars were superseded by patriotic, then by ideological, wars, fought with the same self-immolating loyalty and fervour. The opium of revealed religion was replaced by the heroin of secular religions, which commanded the same bemused surrender of the individuality to their doctrines, and the same worshipful love offered to their prophets. The devils and succubi were replaced by a new demonology: sub-human Jews, plotting world domination; bourgeois capitalists promoting starvation. (238)

Whether it is Nazism or Stalinism, Koestler suggests that the political system perverts what should be the healthy, affective aspects of self-transcendence as part of social integration towards an identificatory myth that blurs the distinctions between reason and unreason. Vaughan, too, is a quasi-political figure insofar as he uses his charm, charisma and sexual presence to bend and manipulate those around him to his apocalyptic myth of the 'coming autogeddon' (*C* 50). He may perform the tender ministrations of a priest, 'he knelt down inside the car and held her face carefully in his hands, whispering into her ear' (*C* 11), but he does so only to add another death to his 'terrifying almanac of … insane wounds' (*C* 13), and to rehearse their final spasms with the prostitutes he collects: 'In the rear seat of the car Vaughan arranged her limbs in the posture of the dying cashier' (*C* 12).

Although there are ready confluences between Jung and Koestler and the evolutionary theories that imbricate Ballard's work, they also exist in dialogue with another psychological strand: behaviourism. As Ballard frequently stated, he had little interest in the individual psychologies of his characters, regarding the concept of personality as at best a humanistic myth. Instead, he was intrigued by the ways in which his characters interacted with an all-pervasive external environment, whether that be the prehistory of the mammalian brain or the unconscious desires projected onto and reflected by the technological domain. Such an approach suggested an affinity with the behavioural psychology of B.F. Skinner whose ideas not only complemented those of cybernetics but also influenced artists working in the wake of the Independent Group, most notably Roy Ascott, Victor Pasmore's protégé and Richard Hamilton's colleague in the fine arts department of Newcastle University (Bracewell 2007, 198–202). It is unclear as to whether Ballard directly knew Skinner's work but the latter's most controversial book, *Beyond Freedom and Dignity*, was released by Ballard's publisher, Jonathan Cape, in 1972.

Skinner (1972, 165–6) not only rejected the humanist belief in individual autonomy but also the attempts of Koestler to regard social dysfunction as human in origin. Nonetheless, like Koestler, Skinner also turned to evolutionary theory for the roots of his critique, arguing that 'culture evolves as new practices arise ... and are selected by their contribution to the strength of the culture as it "competes" with the physical environment and with other cultures' (143). In advocating for 'a technology of behavior' (5), in order to de-escalate real-world threats such as famine, disease, pollution and nuclear war, Skinner regarded his thesis as embroiled in an evolutionary contest with anachronistic yet tenacious concepts such as free will and human inviolability. However, in proposing that the human is no more than the sum of their culture, and cultures are not innate but in constant states of evolution, Skinner argued that both culture and its human products could be re-conditioned: 'explicit design promotes that good by accelerating the evolutionary process, and since a science and a technology of behavior make for better design, they are important "mutations" in the evolution of a culture' (144). It was almost as if Skinner was echoing Lewis's critique of the mechanisation of human behaviour whilst taking *The Art of Being Ruled* as social prescription. Although Skinner acknowledged the comparisons between his model and that of Social Darwinism (132–3), he ultimately glossed over them by reference to a scientifically managed developmental progress (139–43). In other words, Skinner's model lapsed into a form of scientism, the 'dangers' of which were noted by collaborative art practitioners such as Ascott (Bracewell 2007, 201).

With his background in 'the application of computerized techniques to the control of all international traffic systems' (*C* 63), Vaughan is something of a behavioural psychologist. He has a control group of willing subjects, whom he re-conditions through constant surveillance, games and exercises including role-play, the administration of stimuli, and the evaluation of their responses. Vaughan prides himself on being a mentor, and, in James, finds a keen pupil: 'As I embraced Gabrielle I visualized, as Vaughan had taught me, the accidents that might involve the famous and beautiful' (*C* 179). Yet, as Vaughan declines, the relationship evolves so that the tutor relies increasingly on the student: 'Was Vaughan losing his resolve? Already I felt the dominant partner in our relationship' (*C* 190). Does this evolution prove the merits of the behaviourist model or does it indicate the extent to which behaviourism is undermined by the persistence of the reptilian brain? While Vaughan remains fixated on dying with Elizabeth Taylor, the object of his identificatory myth, James's conception of the car crash has turned into something more redemptive: 'the translation of these injuries in terms of our fantasies and sexual behaviour was the only means of re-invigorating these wounded and dying victims' (*C* 190). In other words, whereas Vaughan seeks to transcend his corporeality by fusing his sexuality with that of Taylor's in the violent embrace of the car crash, James seeks to transcend *through* his corporeality—his immanent bodily being—in order to redeem the deaths of countless, unknown crash victims. Having previously sought 'to devise … an even richer exit' for Catherine 'than the death which Vaughan had designed for Elizabeth Taylor' (*C* 181), James concludes his narration by planning 'the elements of my own car-crash' (*C* 224) as a redemptive rather than murderous act.

Nonetheless, the basis for what Ballard called 'a morally justified psychopathology' (*EM* 59) remains ambiguous since, despite embracing their reptilian selves, the protagonists continue to distance themselves from their animal others. And not only non-human animals. The mongrel dog substitutes for the refugees that Helen examines at the immigration centre, its institutional presence reinforcing the all-white, middle-class suburbia as a neo-colonial outpost, while the prostitutes employed on the outskirts of London Airport represent a form of bare life. James mentions biographical details for several of them, suggesting some kind of correspondence other than sexual transaction, but their subjectivities are subordinated to their use-value, primarily for Vaughan's needs. The groundlessness for transcendence is appropriately—and ironically—mediated in animal terms. For Vaughan, the sexual geometry to be found within automobile styling leaves him in 'a trance of recognition, as if he were seeing again some paradise bird' (*C* 170). For James, his pre-existing antipathy for Catherine is symbolised by her representation as 'a hostile and predatory bird' (*C* 195). Although the bird represents flight, to be emulated by James's acid dream of 'a technology with wings' (*C* 209), in each case it also embodies the delusion and paranoia of the male characters. The extent to which female and non-heteronormative sexualities have agency in their own right is the subject of the next chapter.

Works Cited

Barthes, Roland. 1972 (1954). Objective Literature. In *Critical Essays*, trans. Richard Howard, 13–24. Evanston: Northwestern University Press.
Bracewell, Michael. 2007. *Re-make/Re-model: Art, Pop, Fashion and the Making of Roxy Music, 1953–1972*. London: Faber.
Carter, Angela. 1993 (1992). *Expletives Deleted*. London: Vintage.
Chirico, Giorgio de. 1968 (1912). Meditations of a Painter. In *Theories of Modern Art*, ed. Herschel B. Chipp, 397–401. Berkeley: University of California Press.
Conrad, Joseph. 2002 (1900). *Lord Jim*, Ed. Susan Jones. 2nd edn. Ware: Wordsworth Classics.
Foster, Hal. 1991. Armor Fou. *October* 56: 64–97.
Fromm, Erich. 1963 (1956). *The Sane Society*. London: Routledge and Kegan Paul.
Haraway, Donna. 1985. A Manifesto for Cyborgs: Science, Technology, and Socialist Feminism in the 1980s. *Socialist Review* 80: 65–107.
Kavanagh, Ciarán. 2019. Categorically Grotesque: Ballard, Bodies and Genre in *Crash*. *Open Cultural Studies* 3: 456–468.
Koestler, Arthur. 1967. *The Ghost in the Machine*. London: Hutchinson.
Luckhurst, Roger. 1997. *'The Angle Between Two Walls': The Fiction of J.G. Ballard*. Liverpool: Liverpool University Press.
Moore, Erica. 2014. Concrete and Steel Evolution in *Crash*. *Foundation* 119: 41–57.
Murray, Rachel. 2020. *The Modernist Exoskeleton: Insects, War, Literary Form*. Edinburgh: Edinburgh University Press.
Odajnyk, Volodymyr Walter. 1976. *Jung and Politics: The Political and Social Ideas of C.G. Jung*. New York: Harper & Row.
Sage, Victor. 2008. The Gothic, the Body, and the Failed Homeopathy Argument: Reading Crash. In *J.G. Ballard: Contemporary Critical Perspectives*, ed. Jeannette Baxter, 34–49. Manchester: Manchester University Press.
Skinner, B.F. 1972 (1971). *Beyond Freedom and Dignity*. London: Jonathan Cape.
Stephenson, Gregory. 1991. *Out of the Night and Into the Dream: A Thematic Study of the Fiction of J.G. Ballard*. Westport CT: Greenwood Press.
Turgenev, Ivan. 1998 (1862). *Fathers and Sons*. Trans. Richard Freeborn. Oxford: Oxford World's Classics.
Vale, V., ed. 2005. *J.G. Ballard: Conversations*. San Bernadino: Re/Search Publications.
Whiting, Emma. 2012. Disaffection and Abjection in J.G. Ballard's *The Atrocity Exhibition* and *Crash*. In *J.G. Ballard: Visions and Revisions*, ed. Jeannette Baxter and Rowland Wymer, 88–104. Basingstoke: Palgrave Macmillan.
Youngquist, Paul. 2000. Ballard's Crash-Body. *Postmodern Culture* 11.1 (accessed 15/05/24). https://www.pomoculture.org/2013/09/19/ballards-crash-body/

CHAPTER 6

Moral Pornography: Sex, Power and Representation

Abstract This chapter utilises Angela Carter's concept of a 'moral pornography' in order to explore Ballard's representation of women, sexuality and power. Although politically oblique, the novel queers the dominant first-person narration, explicitly, through the portrayal of same-sex desire, and also implicitly, by drawing attention to the subaltern voices at the margins of the central narration. In this regard, comparisons can also be made with other New Wave texts by Michael Moorcock and Joanna Russ.

Keywords Women · Pornography · Homosexuality · Disability · Subalternity

Writing in his synopsis to Tom Maschler, Ballard paid particular attention to the characters of Catherine and Gabrielle. Ballard wrote that the former is 'the very model of a new kind of woman', 'affected, but cool and totally promiscuous'; 'qualities' that the narrator 'admires as they belong to the age of technology'. The latter embodies 'the deformities of flesh and metal', and acts as 'a model for all the possibilities that a deviant technology offers' (*CC*, 10 April 1972). Far from being passengers, women and the differently abled motivate this future landscape since they embody what the male protagonists want to fuse with and become. As avatars, though, of a technological realm that is rapidly engulfing the

© The Author(s), under exclusive license to Springer Nature Switzerland AG 2025
P. March-Russell, *J. G. Ballard's* Crash, Palgrave Science Fiction and Fantasy: A New Canon,
https://doi.org/10.1007/978-3-031-73094-8_6

anthropocentric, the female characters occupy an ambiguous position. Since the car crash is both a destructive and generative act, women are figured as the agents of their own self-destruction, only to be reborn as cyborgs that transcend categories of 'male' and 'female'. The misogyny that underwrites this metamorphosis is complicated by Ballard's knowing use of pornography as a political medium that exposes 'how we use and exploit each other in the most urgent and ruthless way' (*C* 6). This penultimate chapter argues that, just as Ballard was uninterested in cars *per se*, so sex—despite its graphic depiction—is not *Crash*'s *raison d'être*. Instead, it is power, for which the portrayal of queer sexualities forms an integral part.

As David Pringle (1979, 6–10) has observed, Ballard's female characters tend to conform to one of two stereotypes: the self-absorbed or harridan wife, or the femme fatale. In a less sympathetic analysis, Alan McKee (1993) has accused Ballard of a deep-seated sexual unease towards women. Although the roots of this alleged anxiety could be retraced to Ballard's relationship with his 'lively', 'strong-willed' yet 'distant' mother (*ML* 22; 49), such an approach omits the correlation between modernity and female sexuality to be found in Ballard's work. According to postmodernists such as Andreas Huyssen (1986, 47–55), mass culture was regarded by the masculinist discourses of naturalism and modernism as metaphorically feminine: subordinate yet threatening. For the young Ballard, though, US mass culture offered liberation:

> I devoured American comics, which were on sale everywhere in Shanghai and read by all the English boys – *Buck Rogers, Flash Gordon* and, later, *Superman*. Later I read American bestsellers… My parents subscribed to a number of magazines – *Life, Time,* the *New Yorker, Saturday Evening Post* and so on, and I spent hours turning their pages and revelling in their American optimism. (*ML* 20)

As he fantasised on BBC Radio's *Desert Island Discs*, Ballard was entranced by the glamour of screen icons such as Marlene Dietrich, Greta Garbo and Rita Hayworth (Lawley 1992). Although products of the Hollywood system, their visual appearance was less decorative than auratic: a magical presence, both excessively significant and transparently depthless. These cool, commanding, sexually confident women were not only emblematic but embodiments of the cultural commodification that Ballard saw in Shanghai, and which he diagnosed as the coming world order. Vaughan's desire to meld his body with that of Elizabeth Taylor, inheritor to the celluloid divas of Ballard's youth, not only represents his attempt to steal her glamour but to also recreate himself on the other side of the screen as a transcendent, hyperrealistic cyborg.

As both commodities in themselves and personifications of commodity culture, these women are fetishised as objects. In the novel's opening scene, as the reader views Taylor viewing the death scenario imagined for her, whilst in turn being viewed by the onlookers, there appears to be something theatrical when she places 'a gloved hand to her throat' (*C* 7). Yet, to only view this act as a gesture, as a pre-rehearsed and ultimately empty sign, is to deny any agency to Taylor and to see her solely through James's disaffected gaze: an already pornographic representation. This chilling complicity is what the novel enacts over and over again. Driven towards dismantling 'that smothering set of conventions that we call everyday reality' (*RS* 47), the male protagonists posit women as symbolic of some higher truth, yet this narrative account can only end in their erasure: either their literal death or their objectification as a series of malleable, moveable parts. As Susanne Kappeler (1986, 2) argues, 'pornography is not a special case of sexuality; it is a form of representation', and as Ballard observes, bondage has 'nothing to do with sex' but ties the user to 'their own existence ... their own tenancy of time and space' (*RS* 48). In an increasingly abstract and conceptual realm, 'where everything is stylised', sex loses its 'reproductive impulse' and becomes an imaginative exercise: 'there's no longer any reason why intercourse per vagina should be any more satisfying or more desirable ... than say intercourse per anus, per navel or armpit or anything else you care to dream up' (*EM* 34). Ballard queers the sex act by reading it pataphysically—it becomes its own representation—so that pornography, in turn, becomes a key for unlocking this apparently deviant symbolism. Yet, that still leaves the question of who uses and who is used.

In her controversial book, *The Sadeian Woman* (1979), Angela Carter argued that the writings of the Marquis de Sade could be turned against themselves as a device that unlocks the violence of patriarchy and makes space for female sexual desire. At one point, Carter (2001, 19–20) hypothesises what a moral pornography might look like:

> The moral pornographer would be an artist who uses pornographic material as part of the acceptance of the logic of a world of absolute sexual licence for all the genders, and projects a model of the way such a world might work. A

moral pornographer might use pornography as a critique of current relations between the sexes. His business would be the total demystification of the flesh and the subsequent revelation, through the infinite modulations of the sexual act, of the real relations of man and his kind. Such a pornographer would not be the enemy of women, perhaps because he might begin to penetrate to the heart of the contempt for women that distorts our culture even as he entered the realms of true obscenity as he describes it.

Following Carter's intervention, Sam Francis (2008, 152–63) has applied this model to *Crash*, exploring its imbrication of science and pornography, the mistreatment and commodification of the female body, and the desensitising effects upon the characters of mediated sex and violence. He also draws upon Susan Sontag's essay, 'The Pornographic Imagination' (1967), which Ballard first read in book-form in 1969, arguing that both authors regard pornography as 'an exchange economy' (164) of parts and signs:

> It has the power to ingest and metamorphose and translate all concerns that are fed into it, reducing everything into the one negotiable currency of the erotic imperative. All action is conceived as a set of sexual *exchanges*. … The bisexuality, the disregard for the incest taboo, and other similar features common to pornographic narratives function to multiply the possibilities of exchange. Ideally, it should be possible for everyone to have a sexual connection with everyone else. (Sontag 1994, 66–7)

Although Sontag's indefinite series of exchanges, and James's description of 'units in a new currency of pain and desire' (*C* 134), could be grafted onto Jean Baudrillard's empty circuit of interchangeable signs, they can also be read as symptomatic of the 'psychic inflation' discussed in the last chapter: Vaughan's voracious consumption of physical mutilations to service his own overexpanded ego. As Sontag (1994, 70) observes, late capitalism fails 'to provide authentic outlets … for exalted self-transcending modes of concentration and seriousness', and offers instead 'vocabularies of thought and action which are not merely self-transcending but self-destructive'. By this token, Vaughan's obsessive, desperate, and ultimately suicidal actions merely confirm the lack of freedom to be found elsewhere in an increasingly uniform economic order.

However, when critics turn to the question of pornography in *Crash*, they tend to locate Ballard's work alongside familiar sources. As well as Carter and Sontag, Francis refers to Sade and Georges Bataille. Jeannette Baxter (2009, 102–14), in focusing upon Ballard's surrealist lineage, also refers extensively to Bataille—although Ballard admitted to never having read him (*EM* 205–6). What they both disregard is that Sontag spends as much time, if not rather more, discussing Pauline Réage's *Story of O* (1954), which Ballard read as a nineteen-year-old (*RS* 19), than she does Bataille. As Ciarán Kavanagh (2021, 90) warns, the application of pornography as another 'interpretative framework' to reading *Crash* can 'make sense of certain aspects of it, but may fail to provide appropriate context to others, or even provide a context whose inappropriateness is disturbing'. It may be more productive, then, to turn to what Ballard was reading as he finalised the manuscript of *Crash*.

In particular, Ballard owned a copy of Thomas Hess and Linda Nochlin's anthology, *Woman as Sex Object*, which caused some controversy in art circles on its publication in 1972. Like John Berger's (1972, 53–7) contemporaneous distinction between nakedness and nudity, the essays sought to unveil the ideological purposes for which women had been portrayed in art. As Nochlin (1972, 9) declares in the opening essay: 'Whether the erotic object be breast or buttocks, shoes or corsets, a matter of pose or of prototype, the imagery of sexual delight or provocation has always been created *about* women for men's enjoyment, by men.' In prefiguring her celebrated work on the absence of women artists from the (male) canon, Nochlin argues that 'those who have no country have no language. Women have no imagery available – no accepted public language to hand – with which to express their particular viewpoint' (11). For Nochlin, as for the other contributors in the volume, the visual realm of the erotic has been colonised by men, subordinating the experiences of women and disarticulating their expression. This pacification of female desire is reflective of other socio-economic inequalities that subjugate women as a political subject whilst, at the same time, bolstering the male artist's self-image 'as sexually dominant creator ... fashioning from inert matter an ideal erotic object for himself, a woman cut to the very pattern of his desires' (15). Appearing just before the first wave of explicitly feminist art, Nochlin's essay captures a moment of historical tension; significantly, she sees in the work of Sylvia Sleigh (the wife of the Independent Group's Lawrence Alloway) a promising subversion of the gendered conventions between artist and model.

To what extent Ballard would have been influenced, if at all, by Nochlin's essay is difficult to say. He would have been drawn, however, to other pieces in the collection: Marcia Allentuck on Henry Fuseli's Romantic Gothic painting, *The Nightmare* (1781), an object of fascination for the French Surrealists; the paired essays by Martha Kingsbury and Alessandra Comini on late nineteenth-century depictions of the femme fatale in Symbolist art; and Hess's own contribution on the iconography of the pin-up in the work of such artists as Willem de Kooning, Roy Lichtenstein and Robert Rauschenberg. (Most notably, for Ballard, Hess not only refers to Tom Wesselmann's series *The Great American Nude* [1961–1973] but also reproduces Andy Warhol's silkscreen print *Liz* [1963].) Ballard, though, might also have been interested in Gerald Needham's investigation into the influence of pornographic photography on Edouard Manet's painting *Olympia* (1863) and, in much the longest essay in the book, David Kunzle's exploration of the corset as a device that both re-engineers and fetishises the shape and form of the female body. What emerges from all of these texts is the extent to which male artists, in different times and cultures, projected their fears and desires onto the silent woman, constructing competing ideas of the feminine that, quite literally, says more about them than their ostensible subjects.

Despite the presence of this critical scholarship, there is no obvious way in which a similar pro-feminist agenda can be discerned in Ballard's novel. Whilst Ballard had little sympathy for anti-pornography campaigners (*RS* 48), there is little evidence either for the sex-positivity to be found in the work of near-contemporaries, such as social activists like Lynne Segal or US science fiction writers like Samuel R. Delany and Joanna Russ. Sex, like everything else in *Crash*, is instrumentalised; it becomes a means to an end. Nochlin's distinction, however, between the self-serving egotism of the male artist and the expenditure of the pliable, subaltern female opens up a more promising pathway. Nochlin's approach is also complemented by the African-American poet Audre Lorde's (2007, 54) distinction between pornography and eroticism. The former denies the latter since 'it represents the suppression of true feeling' and 'emphasizes sensation' for its own sake. The latter 'is an internal sense of satisfaction to which, once we have experienced it, we know we can aspire.' Eroticism comes from within, and as such, not only empowers women in whatever field or endeavour but also renders them 'dangerous' (55) in the eye of patriarchy. Consequently, pornography acts as a patriarchal instrument in order to alienate women (and, arguably, men) from their erotic selves so as to reinforce the status quo.

Two discourses structure *Crash*. One is that of James whose carefully modulated narration constitutes all that we experience in the novel. His corruptibility is already indicated by the 'minor collision' (*C* 16) that occurs at some unspecified time before the accident that kills Helen's husband. This incident, James recalls, embodies 'the erotic delirium of the car-crash', summed-up by the splash of Catherine's vomit mixed with 'clots of blood like liquid rubies, as viscous and discreet as everything' she produces (*C* 16). Sometime between these two collisions, James becomes 'so excited by the conjunction of an air hostess's fawn gabardine skirt on the escalator in front of me and the distant fuselages of the aircraft' that he 'involuntarily' touches her buttocks (*C* 41). What might be the most torturous excuse possible for an illicit grope is offset by the realisation that James not only insulates his feelings from all others but also from himself. James may refer to the eroticism of the car-crash but he doesn't actually feel it as an internal desire, as Lorde suggests. Instead, his already abstract—and therefore pornographic—response to emotional experience makes James a prime candidate for Vaughan's tutelage.

The other discourse is that of the subaltern voices—the women, the differently abled, the working class, the migrants, the animals—whose expression exists at the margins of James's narration. This distinction is of the utmost importance. Firstly, it reminds the reader that James (the implied author) is not the same as Ballard (the actual author), and that what James expresses is not necessarily what Ballard thinks. Secondly, since there is a distance between Ballard and his fictional alter-ego, it also reminds us that James's narration, although appearing to be all-encompassing, is still subjective. Thirdly, there is a distance between the narrator and the narrated; that what the subaltern voices, from whom we hardly hear, say and mean is distinct from what James tells the reader. Potentially, there is an 'erotic charge' (Lorde 2007, 59) or, in Sontag's terms, sexual exchange that the reader barely notices, but which nonetheless exists, because it lies at the outer edge of James's narration. The unthinking colonialism of such an attitude is expressed not only in Baudrillard's reading of *Crash* but also in the misogyny that predicates his thesis on simulation and pornography:

> There is but one sexuality, one libido – and it is masculine. Sexuality has a strong, discriminative structure centred on the phallus, castration, the Name-of-the-Father, and repression. There is none other. There is no use dreaming of some non-phallic, unlocked, unmarked sexuality. (Baudrillard 1990, 6)

Although in compensation Baudrillard ascribes the ludic performativity of seduction to the feminine, his thesis actively insists upon the necessity of sexual difference since he, like Ballard's male protagonists, is unable to think beyond the masculinist parameters of sexuality. Yet, this limitation can be inferred by what James places at the margins of his narration.

For Brian Baker, the restriction that most clearly defines and restrains *Crash* as a perverse text is its representation of same-sex desire. Drawing upon the work of Jonathan Dollimore, Baker (2000, 85–6) argues that sexual perversity is both defined and contained by its transgression of the sexual norm: in committing what is deemed to be taboo, the perverse act recodifies what passes for normal sexual behaviour. Baker regards all of the aberrant sexual acts described in *Crash* as culminating in James's desire for Vaughan, or more specifically, Vaughan's erotic object: his anus. Once the taboo act of anal penetration has been completed, confirming its perversity in relation to a heterosexual norm, so the logic of heteronormativity is restored: Vaughan kills himself and the final sexual act to be depicted in the novel is between James and Catherine. As Baker writes:

> The act of sodomy in *Crash* does not represent homosexual desire as anything other than a heterosexual perversion: it represents the 'maximum' sexual act, and the *limit* of perversion. It becomes the symbol of a transformative movement towards transcendence, towards rebirth; yet, the anus leads to death. (94)

In other words, even as James explicitly describes his sodomising of Vaughan, the desire that motivates it is contained and ultimately channelled into James's desire for Catherine. As Baker puts it, 'all orifices become' a substitute for 'the vagina' (91). Arguably, though, this displacement is not a symptom of sexual desire, but as with all pornographic representations, a question of power. As James acknowledges, Vaughan's 'attraction lay not so much in a complex of familiar anatomical triggers … but in the stylisation of posture achieved between Vaughan and the car' (*C* 117). The memory of this conjunction is enough for Vaughan to use it as a means of controlling James in the earlier phases of their relationship: 'He knew that as long as he provoked me with his own sex … I would never leave him' (*C* 8). However, as Vaughan deteriorates, the sex act becomes James's means for appropriating the 'sexual authority' (*C* 147) that Vaughan had previously extended over him. In their coupling, James not only takes the lead but also effectively feminises Vaughan, first by recalling his sexual encounters with Catherine, Helen and Gabrielle, and then by describing Vaughan pejoratively as 'a deranged drag queen revealing the leaking scars of an unsuccessful trans-sexual surgery' (*C* 201). In the calm that follows, the two men show each other their wounds, 'exposing the scars on our chests and hands to the beckoning injury sites of the car' (*C* 203), as if commemorating not only the camaraderie of their battle-worn bodies but also those killed (and those to die) on the motorised battlefield. Questions of desire and power are therefore sublimated within a code of brotherhood that not only invokes such classical pairings as Achilles and Patroclus or David and Jonathan, but also Shakespeare's *Henry V* (1599), a masculine code that Ballard would have known only too well from his private school education, let alone Laurence Olivier's wartime adaptation. In recalling that Vaughan was modelled on Christopher Evans, Charles Platt (2012, 15) notes there was something 'amazingly British' in Ballard writing 'a novel in which you describe yourself inserting your penis in the rectum of your closest pal, and then continue your friendship without either person saying a word about it'.

This sublimation not only converts the violence of other encounters into an act of tenderness, James seeks 'not to injure' Vaughan (*C* 202), but it also neutralises the 'psychic dislocation' that Sontag (1994, 47) associates with pornography; Vaughan is positioned as the calm 'eye' (*C* 200) of the psychedelic storm that rages around James. In addition, the writing, already teetering on the edges of what we might mean by genre, becomes even less science-fictional since, as Sontag (1994, 47) observes, SF is geared, like pornography, towards 'disorientation'. The 'dreamlike landscape' and 'congealed time', if not 'the spaceships and teeming planets' (46), which Sontag associates with the iconography of SF, sound almost like a summary of Ballard's early short stories. But here, although a hallucinogenic dream orbits James's consciousness, the description of his sex act with Vaughan is conveyed with tender realism. The reader is not so much disoriented as asked to reorient themselves in terms of the visibility of the sexual act. As Linda Williams (1999, 304) argues, *contra* Baudrillard, 'in pornography, the human body is never superfluous'. Yet, this tonal re-registering is not atypical of New Wave texts, for example, the homosexual encounters in Michael Moorcock's *Breakfast in the Ruins* (1972) occur outside of the main time-travelling narrative whilst, in Russ's *The Female Man* (1975), Joanna's seduction of Laura is described with the most delicate and sympathetic realism. Over and above the New Wave's characteristic interrogation of generic borders, what these scenes amount to, even the *liebestod* of James's encounter with Vaughan, is another kind of imagining within the narrow parameters of masculinist or heterosexist discourse. For Ballard, whose own views of homosexuality, despite his admiration for William Burroughs and Jean Genet, were often quite reticent, the constant 'moral challenge' (*EM* 189) of writing *Crash* compelled him to think more deeply about his own beliefs.

To some extent, Baker's definition of both hetero- and homosexuality in terms of the sex act leads him to overlook the queer effects that occur throughout the novel. If sex is not defined in terms of either anal or vaginal penetration, then instead of a series of heteronormative substitutions, both sex and sexuality are radically queered. This queering is most clearly seen in James's encounter with Gabrielle. Carolyn Lau's recent intervention supplants the postmodern emphasis upon the conceptualised body with a focus on the materiality of flesh as derived from disability studies. In emphasising that the able-bodied James must adapt to Gabrielle's specially fitted car rather than the other way around, Lau (2024, 103) argues that Gabrielle's pursuit of 'pleasure through perversity' not only asserts her own needs as a disabled person but also exposes the hypocrisies of ableist normativity. However, Lau glosses over the pejorative descriptions that occur elsewhere in James's narration: his references to 'autistic children crushed in rear-end collisions, their eyes less wounded in death' (*C* 15) or 'the exaggerated pirouette of a mentally defective girl' (*C* 22). Despite the 'ordeals' (*C* 176) that James must pass in order to satisfy Gabrielle, he nonetheless sees himself as teaching her about 'the new parameters of her body, developing a sexual expertise that would be an exact analogue of the other skills created by the multiplying technologies of the twentieth century' (*C* 100). What James discovers is that 'the nominal junction points of the sexual act' (*C* 178) fail to excite her. Far more enticing 'than the membrane of a vagina' is Gabrielle's deep thigh wound, into which James first ejaculates; a 'depraved orifice, the invagination of a sexual organ still in the embryonic stages of its evolution' (*C* 177). During their encounters, James ejaculates into the other 'abstract vents' torn open in Gabrielle's body, whilst also imagining how 'this repertory of orifices' could be expanded in relation 'to the ever-more complex technologies of the future' (*C* 179). Crucially, these 'auxiliary orifices' carved into the body or 'fitted' like prostheses would be 'neither vagina nor rectum' (*C* 180); an unprecedented, decidedly queer erotic object that reassembles the body as an extension of the technological apparatus. In using Gabrielle and then Catherine as templates for this imaginary sexual exchange, James resembles Nochlin's male artist, who treats female flesh as 'inert matter … cut to the very pattern of his desires'.

Although Gabrielle embodies the transhuman ideal of the cyborg, her queerness is both appropriated and instrumentalised by James in order to perpetuate a fixation upon the phallus. This illusory power, though, is contrasted with the lesbian desire that surfaces at the edges of James's discourse. Catherine teases with the concept, primarily in her flirtatious relationship with her secretary, as a stimulus for achieving orgasm with James. As he puts it, these 'elaborate' fantasies appear 'to be a language in search of objects' (*C* 35). Instead, the homosexual 'streak' (*C* 33) that James imputes to Catherine is evident in himself since he has already had a 'relationship with a young mezzanine bartender' (*C* 41). James's disavowal of his sexual tendencies may, in part, explain his ridicule of the idea of 'lesbian supermarket manageresses burning to death in … their midget cars' (*C* 15). At the end of his narrative, though, James approves of Helen's growing perversity as she finds 'happiness' in Gabrielle's 'gentle embraces' (*C* 223–4), suggesting that she—unlike James—is ideally adapted for this cyborg future. Nonetheless, their sudden appearance is neither foreshadowed nor explained in James's narration, so that this lesbian pairing seems both utopian and incredible.

Alternatively, the lack of explanation queers the causal links in the elliptical narration, so that their relationship not only foregrounds the limitations in James's discourse but also poses an answer to the object-less language for which James can only see some far-off 'physical expression' (*C* 35). The absence of any lesbian sex in this otherwise graphic account suggests not only James's lack of intuition but also its escape from the pornographic gaze. Whereas male homosexual desire can be reconstituted within the power structures that determine the heterosexual hegemony, lesbianism slips its objectification. If, as a consequence, lesbian desire appears to be mute, at least Ballard acknowledges that there are aspects of human experience, and hence potential sources of power, that cannot be voiced by James's framing narrative or taxonomised by Vaughan's compulsive collection. Such questions would have to be addressed by the feminist SF of the 1970s, but the extent to which *Crash* is at least in dialogue with those questions may also explain why, in more recent years, it has been taken up by younger female artists.

Works Cited

Baker, Brian. 2000. The Resurrection of Desire: J.G. Ballard's *Crash* as a Transgressive Text. *Foundation* 80: 84–97.
Baudrillard, Jean. 1990 (1979). *Seduction*. Trans. Brian Singer. Basingstoke: Macmillan.
Baxter, Jeannette. 2009. *J.G. Ballard's Surrealist Imagination: Spectacular Authorship*. Farnham: Ashgate.
Berger, John. 1972. *Ways of Seeing*. London: BBC/Penguin.
Carter, Angela. 2001 (1979). *The Sadeian Woman: An Exercise in Cultural History*. London: Penguin.
Francis, Sam. 2008. "Moral Pornography" and "Total Imagination": The Pornographic in J.G. Ballard's *Crash*. *English* 218: 146–168.
Huyssen, Andreas. 1986. *After the Great Divide: Modernism, Mass Culture, Postmodernism*. Bloomington: Indiana University Press.
Kappeler, Susanne. 1986. *The Pornography of Representation*. Cambridge: Polity.
Kavanagh, Ciarán. 2021. Refiguring Reader-Response: Experience and Interpretation in J.G. Ballard's *Crash*. In *Powerful Prose: How Textual Features Impact Readers*, ed. R.L. Victoria Pöhls and Mariane Utudji, 77–95. Bielefeld: transcript Verlag.
Lau, Carolyn. 2024. *Posthuman Subjectivity in the Novels of J.G. Ballard*. New York: Routledge.
Lawley, Sue. 1992. *Desert Island Discs*. BBC Radio 4, August 30. https://www.bbc.co.uk/programmes/p0093yf6 (accessed 03/06/24).
Lorde, Audre. 2007 (1984). *Sister Outsider*. Berkeley: Crossing Press.
McKee, Alan. 1993. Intentional Phalluses: The Male "Sex" in J.G. Ballard. *Foundation* 57: 58–68.
Nochlin, Linda. 1972. Eroticism and Female Imagery in Nineteenth-Century Art. In *Woman as Sex Object: Studies in Erotic Art, 1730–1970*, ed. Thomas B. Hess and Linda Nochlin, 8–15. New York: Newsweek.
Platt, Charles. 2012. New Worlds for Old, 1965–1970. *Relapse* 20: 11–19.
Pringle, David. 1979. The Lamia, the Jester and the King: J.G. Ballard's Characters. *Foundation* 16: 4–15.
Sontag, Susan. 1994 (1969). *Styles of Radical Will*. London: Vintage.
Williams, Linda. 1999. *Hard Core: Power, Pleasure, and the 'Frenzy of the Visible'*. 2nd ed. Berkeley: University of California Press.

CHAPTER 7

Coda: Autogeddon/Anthropocene

Abstract Whilst acknowledging Ballard's eco-scepticism, the coda argues that *Crash*'s apocalypticism finds affinities with the 'dark ecology' of such philosophers as Timothy Morton. The coda focuses on the unconscious Anthropocenic logic to be found in the novel and suggests that, whilst James's narration embodies a terminal condition, the subaltern voices at its margins represent the endurance of life after the apocalypse.

Keywords Environmentalism • Ecology • Waste • Apocalypse • Anthropocene

Ballard once commented that he was 'completely out of sympathy with the whole antitechnology movement':

> Everything from the Club of Rome on the one hand to Friends of the Earth on the other ... their prescriptions for disaster always strike me as simply wrong ... and also appallingly defeatist... I feel very *optimistic* about science and technology. And yet almost my entire fiction has been an illustration of the opposite. (*DM* 89)

Despite recent ecocritical attempts to reclaim Ballard's fiction (Knowles 2018), his scepticism remained intact, manifesting in such late satires as

Rushing to Paradise (1994). For Ballard, the ascent of the technological landscape at the expense of the natural world was inevitable, and, if anything, should be encouraged. Jousting with his friend, the writer and psychogeographer Iain Sinclair, Ballard argued that the English were still living in a wartime mentality where 'pleasure should be rationed':

> They feel that the freedom and ability that a six-lane highway brings is something to disapprove of. So any legislation aimed at restricting the motor car meets with a sort of knee-jerk attraction of approval. We need more roads. Concrete in the whole of southern England. After all … the so-called countryside that people rhapsodise about doesn't really exist. (Sinclair 2002)

The apparent perversity of Ballard's response, though, is consonant with James's desire in *Crash* to release the frustrated motorists from their continual traffic jams, not by retreating into an infantile Romantic pastoralism (as Wyndham Lewis might have put it), but by taking the logic of the car to its ultimate ends and merging with the machine in a violent, libidinal discharge. For Ballard, such an ending is both generative and optimistic since it negates both the futility of repression and the compromise of sublimation. In becoming other, the self—in Ballard's logic—finds a psychic unity that goes beyond anthropocentric notions of good and evil, life and death.

As such, *Crash* resonates with the 'dark ecology' of philosophers such as Timothy Morton (2016) for whom the world has already ended, that is to say, the world as defined from the human point of view. The planet, a separate and irreducible entity to human understanding, will continue with or without us: a maddening thought, as Ballard suggests, for the inflated ego that results in 'the determination to bring about its destruction' (*UG* 208). Quoting the psychoanalyst Edward Glover, in this same 1977 essay on apocalypses, Ballard regards the ego's inability to accept its finitude as the basis for the sadism that ultimately manifests in nuclear war, or indeed, Vaughan's authoritarian and sociopathic behaviour. By contrast, the translation of such impulses into art 'represents a constructive and positive act': 'in the cataclysm story the science fiction writer [uses] his imagination to describe the infinite alternatives to reality' which, for Ballard, constitutes a 'celebration of the possibilities of life' (*UG* 208–9). Whether this life is human, posthuman or in any shape anthropocentric is another matter altogether.

7 CODA: AUTOGEDDON/ANTHROPOCENE

Whatever else *Crash* offers, it is not the spectacularised body of postmodern theory but a heterogeneous entity characterised by waste, detritus and mess. For Jeannette Baxter (2009, 103), the novel features an economy of 'blood, semen, shit and pus' that foregrounds both the contingency of social structures and the fragility of human bodies. For Rachele Dini (2016, 135), the waste products of flesh and metal indicate 'the irrationality underlying consumer culture', whilst Dominika Oramus (2015, 131) dwells upon the profane beauty of 'broken glass' that glitters within garbage-strewn roads and pavements. This illumination, though, presages both the most science-fictional and the most global insight in the whole narrative:

> Within fifty years, as more and more cars collided here, the glass fragments would form a sizable bar, within thirty years a beach of sharp crystal. A new race of beachcombers might appear, squatting on these heaps of fractured windshields, sifting them for cigarette butts, spent condoms and loose coins. Buried beneath this new geological layer laid down by the age of the automobile accident would be my own small death, as anonymous as a vitrified scar in a fossil tree. (*C* 56–7)

In imagining a fresh geological stratum to be surveyed by a posthuman species, hunting for the discarded remnants of what they vaguely know as human civilisation, James offers a striking image for both the Anthropocene and its apocalyptic aftermath. Whilst *Crash* is sometimes regarded as not even science fiction, or at best a science fiction of the near-future, here James can only turn to SF imagery in order to fully think through the implications of where the autogeddon might lead. Embedded within this retrospective text is a sense of deep time that, like the evolutionary elements discussed previously, places the narrative into a historically wider, geographically larger and politically more uncertain landscape. For Vaughan, each crash victim is 'fossilized for ever' in a 'web of chromium knives and frosted glass' (*C* 12), an eternal preservation that suggests redemption, but which also implies a new 'web' of life that has been re-engineered and re-hybridised by the coagulation of flesh, metal and glass. As Mark Bould (2021, 78) remarks, 'Ballard rejects vertical hierarchies in favour of a lateral dissolution of boundaries'. James's narration, in seeking to enframe and englobe, reveals its own contradictions by incorporating a post-apocalyptic scenario that includes post-Anthropocenic humans, who are undefined by what we have done to the planet with our cars, our technologies, our sadisms, and who are adapted to survive in whatever comes after whereas James, and the culture he embodies, is no more than an indistinguishable fossil.

In the same year as *Crash* was published, Richard Mabey produced *The Unofficial Countryside*, the precursor to the new nature writing of such authors as Roger Deakin, Tim Dee, Helen Macdonald and Robert Macfarlane. Built around a series of walks over a twelve-month period, Mabey's book scanned the edgelands of west London, discovering the flora and fauna that had emerged in the cracks of an increasingly urbanised and motorised landscape. It was, as Sinclair (2010, 12) has noted, the counterpart to *Crash*:

> Ballard's perverse (but tender) ecology of petrol, blood, semen, crumpled metal, is the soundtrack playing at the edge of Mabey's frame as he logs willowherbs, mosses and knotgrass. Mabey's rogue plants, scuttling creatures migrating along central reservations and colonising abandoned filling stations, are the local jungle into which Ballard's architect, Robert Maitland, plunges in *Concrete Island*.

Despite the global climate emergency, urban nature continues to adapt and survive, almost in a mirror-image to Ballard's prognostications upon the future of humans and machines. If his claim that the suburban hinterland as the site of cultural innovation holds any substance, then it follows that what lies at the margins of James's narration, in the spaces between human and non-human habitation, is another life-force which James barely notices but which Mabey sensitively describes. Yet, it also follows that this life exists on the borders of James's narration like the novel's other subaltern voices. Whether *Crash* acknowledges them or not, they nonetheless persist, like Mabey's wild flowers and animals, in the interstices of the built environment. They too speak to 'the possibilities of life'.

Works Cited

Baxter, Jeannette. 2009. *J.G. Ballard's Surrealist Imagination: Spectacular Authorship*. Farnham: Ashgate.

Bould, Mark. 2021. *The Anthropocene Unconscious: Climate Catastrophe Culture*. London: Verso.

Dini, Rachele. 2016. Waste in J.G. Ballard's Urban Disaster Trilogy. In *Deep Ends 3*, ed. Rick McGrath, 130–143. Toronto: Terminal Press.

Knowles, Thomas, ed. 2018. J.G. Ballard and the Natural World. Special issue of *Green Letters* 22.4.

Morton, Timothy. 2016. *Dark Ecology: For a Logic of Future Coexistence*. Columbia: Columbia University Press.

Oramus, Dominika. 2015 (2007). *Grave New World: The Decline of the West in the Fiction of J.G. Ballard*. Toronto: Terminal Press.

Sinclair, Iain. 2002. Why the Future Goes Round in Circles. *The Daily Telegraph*, October 19.

———. 2010. Introduction to Richard Mabey. In *The Unofficial Countryside*, 7–13. Toller Fratrum: Little Toller Books.

Index[1]

A
Aldiss, Brian, 33, 37, 38, 58
Alloway, Lawrence, 47, 48, 50, 73
Ambit, 32, 33
Animals, 59, 60, 67, 75, 84
Anthropocene, 81–84
Anthropology, 43–54
Apocalypse, 82
Ascott, Roy, 65, 66
Augé, Marc, 44
Authoritarian personality
    charisma, 52, 65
    seduction, 53

B
Ballard, J.G., 1, 2, 4–7, 7n1, 9–19, 20n5, 20n7, 23–38, 39n1, 39n2, 43–51, 53, 54, 55n1, 55n2, 57–63, 65–67, 69–79, 81–84
The Atrocity Exhibition, 2, 6, 7n2, 11, 25–29, 32, 33, 36, 43, 51, 52
Concrete Island, 6, 15, 84
Crash! (drama-documentary), 17
'Crash' (stage show), 33
'Crashed Cars' (exhibition), 34
The Crystal World, 11, 61
The Drowned World, 11, 62, 63
Empire of the Sun, 6, 38
'The Innocent as Paranoid,' 17, 37
The Kindness of Women, 6, 35, 36
'The Terminal Beach,' 24
Ballard, Mary, 25, 26, 31
Banham, Reyner, 47
Bataille, Georges, 48, 72, 73
Baudrillard, Jean, 16–18, 20n6, 20n7, 30, 38, 39n1, 44, 72, 75–77
Burroughs, William, 12, 16, 24, 25, 31, 37, 78

---

[1] Note: Page numbers followed by 'n' refer to notes.

© The Author(s), under exclusive license to Springer Nature Switzerland AG 2025
P. March-Russell, *J. G. Ballard's* Crash, Palgrave Science Fiction and Fantasy: A New Canon,
https://doi.org/10.1007/978-3-031-73094-8

INDEX

C
Canon, 3, 4, 6, 73
Carter, Angela, 51, 55n2, 59, 71, 72
Charli XCX, 1
Cokeliss, Harley, 17, 26, 29, 30, 35, 36
Collage, 24, 46, 53, 54
Colonialism, 75
Commodity, 30, 45, 50, 51, 53, 71
Consumerism, 18, 45, 46, 48
Crash (compositional history)
 blurb, 14, 17
 cautionary warning, 17
 death of affect, 18, 33, 47
 editing, 43
 French introduction, 12, 13, 16, 33, 36, 37
 jacket design, 13
 marketing, 13
 reader's report, 9
 reviews, 14, 15, 17, 20n3, 35, 36
 synopsis, 14, 33, 34
Cronenberg, David, 1, 7n1
Cybernetics, 47, 55n1, 58, 65
Cyberpunk, 16, 19, 38
Cyborg, 1, 31, 57–67, 70, 71, 79

D
Disability, 78
Drake, Gabrielle, 36
Ducournau, Julia, 1

E
Ecology, 36, 84
England, 5, 26, 44–46, 82
Evans, Christopher, 31, 32, 34, 35, 77
Evolution, 62, 66, 78

F
Flaubert, Gustave, 38, 58
Freud, Sigmund, 27, 30

G
Gascoyne, David, 49
Genet, Jean, 12, 16, 31, 78

H
Hamilton, Richard, 46, 47, 65
Hemingway, Ernest, 33, 61
Henderson, Nigel, 47, 49
Homosexuality, 78

I
Immanence, 60–62
Imperialism, 51
The Independent Group (IG), 5, 43–54, 65, 73
 This is Tomorrow, 46
Institute for Contemporary Arts (ICA), 31, 33, 34, 46
 Cybernetic Serendipity, 33, 34
Intersectionality, 6, 7
Ionesco, Eugène, 34

J
Jarry, Alfred, 28–31, 37, 39n1
 pataphysics, 28, 39n1
Jung, Carl, 63–65
 psychic inflation, 64

K
Koestler, Arthur, 46, 64–66
 brain development, 64
 identificatory myth, 65, 67

Kulowski, Jacob, 32, 54
Kustow, Mike, 33

L
Lesbianism, 79
Lewis, Wyndham, 30, 31, 37, 38, 39n2, 63, 66, 82
Lorde, Audre, 74, 75
Lotringer, Sylvère, 16
Luckhurst, Roger, 4, 5, 19, 38, 54, 60

M
Mabey, Richard, 84
MacBeth, George, 32
Madge, Charles, 49, 50
Maschler, Tom, 5, 10–15, 17, 69
Mass Observation (MO), 44, 48–50, 54
McLuhan, Marshall, 30
Modernism, 23–39, 46, 59, 70
Moorcock, Michael, 16, 24, 25, 28, 32, 33, 37, 38, 39n2, 47, 77
  Breakfast in the Ruins, 77
  Jerry Cornelius (character), 28
  New Worlds, 24, 25, 27, 28, 32, 34, 37, 39n2, 47, 48
  The Sundered Worlds, 28

N
Nader, Ralph, 12, 26
New Arts Lab, 34, 35, 47
New Wave, 5, 16, 37, 77
Nicholls, Peter, 37
Nietzsche, Friedrich, 28
Nouveau roman, 58

P
Paolozzi, Eduardo, 25, 32, 37, 39, 46–48
Peters, Catherine, 10, 11, 13, 14

Petty, Mike, 11, 13, 20n1
Platt, Charles, 47, 77
Pornography, 5, 15, 16, 69–79
Posthuman, 5, 82, 83
Postmodernism, 16, 18, 27, 28
Priestley, J.B., 45, 46
Punk, 15, 16

R
Réage, Pauline, 12, 16, 73
Russ, Joanna, 74, 77

S
Skinner, B.F., 65, 66
  behaviourism, 65, 67
Sontag, Susan, 19, 30, 72, 73, 75, 77
Stanley, Jo, 35
Storr, Anthony, 10
Subaltern, 36, 50, 74, 75, 84
Suburbia, 4, 43, 44, 53, 67
Surrealism, 5, 39, 43–54

T
Tennant, Emma, 11
Transcendence, 18, 29, 60–62, 67, 76
Transhuman, 79

V
Vale, V., 16, 64

W
Walsh, Claire, 32
Waste, 83
Woman as Sex Object (Hess and Nochlin), 73

Z
Zoline, Pamela, 34, 37, 47

SPRINGER NATURE

GPSR Compliance

The European Union's (EU) General Product Safety Regulation (GPSR) is a set of rules that requires consumer products to be safe and our obligations to ensure this.

If you have any concerns about our products, you can contact us on ProductSafety@springernature.com

In case Publisher is established outside the EU, the EU authorized representative is:

Springer Nature Customer Service Center GmbH
Europaplatz 3
69115 Heidelberg, Germany

The manufacturer's authorised representative in the EU is Springer Nature Customer Service Centre GmbH, Europaplatz 3, 69115 Heidelberg, Germany. If you have any concerns regarding our products, please contact ProductSafety@springernature.com

Printed and bound by CPI Group (UK) Ltd, Croydon, CR0 4YY

20/11/2025

02001868-0002